21st CENTURY GUIDE TO BUILDING YOUR VOCABULARY

TEST YOURSELF—

1. Would you be comfortable using the word "interminable" in a sentence?

2. How should you respond if someone calls you "amicable"?

3. Should you worry more if the doctor says you have a "hematoma" or a "hemorrhage"?

4. If someone suggests you eat *al fresco,* should you expect pasta?

5. You can use the high-quality company _____ for those important reports.   (a) stationary   (b) stationery

---

1. "Interminable" means unending. A boring meeting or a bad movie or a visit from a relative can seem "interminable."
2. It means "friendly," so you should feel complimented.
3. Hematoma only means a bruise, hemorrhage means bleeding.
4. Nope, just expect to be outside.
5. (b) stationery

FOR FAST, FOCUSED RESULTS
YOU CAN INCORPORATE IN YOUR DAILY
COMMUNICATIONS . . .

—21ST— CENTURY GUIDE TO BUILDING YOUR VOCABULARY

EDITED BY THE PRINCETON LANGUAGE INSTITUTE

ELIZABETH READ, COMPILER

ELLEN LICHTENSTEIN, SPECIAL CONSULTANT

PRODUCED BY THE PHILIP LIEF GROUP, INC.

A DELL BOOK

Published by
Dell Publishing
a division of
Random House, Inc.
1540 Broadway
New York, New York 10036

Published by arrangement with
The Philip Lief Group, Inc.
6 West 20 Street
New York, New York 10011

ISBN 978-0-440-61368-8

Published simultaneously in Canada

Contents

Introduction   **vii**

**1. Dialogue: The Communication
   Process**   **1**

Strategies for Improving Communication
   Skills   1
The Protocol of Language   2
Functional vs. Recognition Vocabulary   3
Essential Vocabulary I   5

**2. Unlocking Meaning: The Components
   of English Words**   **23**

Prefixes   25
Suffixes   31
Other Word Components   34
Essential Vocabulary II   57

**3. Spinning Off: Increasing Your
   Functional Vocabulary**   **69**

Changing Word Components   69
Essential Vocabulary III   75

4. English: A Rich and Varied Language   99

Foreign Terms   101
Abbreviations   110
Words from Literature, Mythology,
    and History   112
Essential Vocabulary IV   117

5. English: Today's Global Language   133

The Word Components of Medicine   135
The Language of Law   141
The Language of Technology,
    Science, and Medicine   147
The Language of Business, Society,
    and Politics   155
Essential Vocabulary V   165

6. Fine-tuning: Final Challenges   179

Problems with Verb Forms   179
Irregular and Unusual Plurals   183
Problem Word Pairs   185

Review Drills   197

Introduction

In the 21st century, rapid and clear communication will be the critical factor in all facets of life — business, government, education, the sciences. Those who succeed and excel will be those with the communication skills that get their message across clearly, succinctly, and thoroughly to every kind of listener or reader. This book will equip you with the tools you need — cutting-edge vocabulary, an understanding of the basic communication process, and approaches to fine-tuning your communication skills.

USING THIS BOOK

The most effective language-learning techniques are used in this book. We provide a regular pattern throughout each section of new material and immediate drills. In the drills, newly introduced material is interwoven with material presented in earlier sections. Answer keys are provided immediately after each drill, to reinforce your increasing self-confidence and retention.

As an added vocabulary-building aid, an Essential Vocabulary list is supplied as the final section of each of the first five chapters. Again, try to learn a few new words from these essential vocabulary lists each time you open the book, and test your growing skills as you work your way through each section. Along with the specialized vocabulary lists in Chapters 4 and 5, these higher level words are ones you should try to incorporate into your daily communication, thereby increasing your recognition vocabulary naturally.

—21ST—
CENTURY
GUIDE TO
BUILDING YOUR
VOCABULARY

1

Dialogue
The Communication Process

STRATEGIES FOR IMPROVING COMMUNICATION SKILLS

Words are the tools of thought: they are not only the means by which we express specific ideas but also the vehicle through which we express reality as we perceive it. Simply put, the more words you have at your command, the better able you are to express fine facets of reality. And the most dynamic, effective language for expression is English — English has more words, more synonyms, than any other language past or present. So, if you are able to deepen and broaden your command of English, you will be equipped to understand and express the more subtle aspects of life and thought.

Powerful speakers and writers are able to express themselves economically — they say much in few words. They don't need to beat around the bush, talking around the subject because they can't find exactly the right word. They literally compress meaning into one powerful word choice. They use simple, direct eloquence, not high-blown, intimidating language, to motivate and communicate. Effective communication means being understood by your listener or reader. True genius is being able to express complex thoughts in simple, understandable language, and only someone with true command of the English language can do that.

So, how do you decide which word to use?

1. **Understand your audience's level of sophistication:** What is their level of comprehension? You would explain chicken pox to a child much differently than you would to a gathering of physicians. Knowing your audience will guide you in how much detail to provide and how thoroughly you need to explain an idea.

2. **Understand your audience's frame of reference:** Talking about "CDs" and "principal" with a banker is going to mean something very different from talking about "CDs" to a musical producer and talking about "principal" to an elementary schoolteacher.

3. **Understand your audience's relationship to you:** The exchange of information must be shaped according to the appropriateness of the language. Using slang with your supervisor and using stiff oratorical language with your toddler prevent effective communication.

THE PROTOCOL OF LANGUAGE

According to some communication experts, English has five different levels of formality: oratorical (formal speeches, as in politics); deliberative (large audience, informative content, as in teaching); consultative (one-on-one, but still formal, as with one's doctor); casual (friends, peers); and intimate (close family and friends). In these, word choice, emotional content, and delivery style range from cold/abstract to warm/concrete.

It is absolutely essential, if you are to communicate effectively, that you understand the subtleties of the communication process. *How* you say something is sometimes more important than *what* is actually said. Your word choices and delivery "style" must be geared according to your audience's information needs, comprehension level, and relationship to you personally.

Let's take a simple example:

1. "She's hit the sack."
2. "Gerry's gone to bed."
3. "Ms. Conroy has retired for the evening."

All three sentences are expressing exactly the same incident, but clearly they are expressing very different messages about the audience receiving the information. Number 1 is very informal, highly imagistic, clearly intended for a close relationship. Number 2 is still familiar, but more straightforward, perhaps intended for a friend or neighbor. Number 3 is stiff, impersonal, abstract. A remote business associate calling on the telephone might be given this message, but certainly not a close relative.

In any case, had the wrong message been delivered to the wrong audience, the emotional impact would have been powerful — and the importance of the information would have been lost.

As our communication becomes increasingly international and instantaneous, understanding this simple concept — know your audience — becomes as important as increasing the depth of your recognition vocabulary.

FUNCTIONAL VS. RECOGNITION VOCABULARY

It is a well-established fact that there is a critical relationship between personal and professional success and effective communication skills. This book will reveal the steps and techniques needed to do just that. Listen carefully to powerful speakers—they don't use difficult language and fancy vocabularies. They speak in simple, clear, and precise language. They have the entire language at their command because they know exactly which word to choose to express their thoughts to any audience.

Learn to figure out the meaning of new words by understanding how they are used in a sentence—is it a verb? does it have a positive or negative sense? can you "dissect" the word to learn its meaning? Begin to think visually—by learning the word components and focusing on their visual meanings, you can better remember new words. By learning the techniques of spinning off meanings presented in this book, you can clearly double your functional vocabulary.

What exactly is a *functional* vocabulary? It is those words you use and understand every day, the words you are comfortable with and rely on to express your thoughts. The key is to expand your functional vocabulary to incorporate those words now in your *recognition* vocabulary—those new or higher level words you hear and read, but don't use or understand perfectly. This is the secret of a truly powerful 21st century vocabulary.

As you become more tuned in to the communication needs of your audience, you will automatically choose your words more carefully. To do this, you need to be able to select synonyms and antonyms rapidly and precisely. Learning the interrelated word components presented in this book and the techniques for spinning off new words will give you that capability.

ESSENTIAL VOCABULARY I

A

abate	to lessen in amount, degree, or force
abbreviate	to shorten
aberration	exception or departure from what is true, normal, or correct
abet	to tolerate or encourage a criminal act
abeyance	temporary suspension or holding-off
abhor	to despise, detest, hold in disgust
abject	miserable, wretched
abnegate	to renounce, deny, and refuse for oneself
abolish	to cancel, do away with
abominate	to loathe, hate
abortive	unsuccessful, fruitless
abrasive	annoyingly harsh or aggressive; scraping
abridge	to shorten, edit out
abrogate	to annul, cancel
abscond	to steal and flee
absolution	forgiveness; freeing from guilt or obligation
abstain	to refrain from or hold oneself back
abstruse	difficult to understand; complex or deep
abut	joined end to end
accede	to attain to or enter upon duties or responsibilities
accelerate	to go faster
acclaim	to applaud, greet with approval

acclivity	upward slope
accolade	praise; award
accumulate	to gather over time
accustom	to familiarize by habit or repetition
acerbity	sourness; bitter or astringent
acme	the top or highest point
acolyte	assistant, usually in a religious ceremony
acquiesce	to give in to, agree to without protest
acquit	to discharge from obligation; to set free
acrimony	bitterness or harshness of temper, manner, or speech
actuary	person who calculates insurance risks
actuate	to put into action or motion
acumen	shrewdness, keenness, quickwittedness
adage	proverb, wise saying
adamant	hard, firm, inflexible
adduce	to provide as a reason or example
adept	skilled, expert at something
adhere	to stick to, stay attached to
adipose	fatty
adjunct	something added onto something; secondary but not essential
admonish	to warn, caution against
adroit	skillful, clever
adulation	flattery, servile praise
adumbration	obscured, overshadowed
adventitious	accidental, serendipitous

adverse	contrary, oppositional
adversity	misfortune; poverty
advocate	to defend, plead, or urge for another's cause
aesthetic	artistic; sensitive to beauty and the arts
affable	friendly, pleasant, easy to talk to
affidavit	sworn written statement
affiliation	connection to or association with a group or organization
affinity	relationship; kinship
affirmation	assertion; solemn vow or declaration
affluent	wealthy; plentiful, abundant
aggravate	to trouble, make worse or difficult
aggregate	the total, whole
agitate	to stir up, shake up; to cause dissension
agnostic	person who does not think it possible to know whether or not a God exists
agoraphobia	fear of open spaces
agronomy	science of crop production and soil management
alacrity	quickness; liveliness; briskness
alienate	to estrange, make unfriendly
allay	to pacify, calm, put fears to rest
alleviate	to lighten or relieve pain, suffering, or difficulty
allocate	to allot, distribute according to a plan
allude	to refer to indirectly, suggest
aloof	standoffish; removed
altercation	argument, dispute

altruism	selfless concern for others
amalgamate	to combine, unite
amass	to pile up, stockpile
ambidextrous	able to use both hands with equal ease and skill
ambiguous	having more than one possible meaning
ambivalent	having simultaneously conflicting or contradictory feelings
ambulatory	able to work
ameliorate	to improve, make better
amenable	agreeable; able to be controlled or influenced
amicable	peaceable, friendly; showing goodwill
amoral	incapable of distinguishing between what is morally right and wrong
amulet	charm worn to protect against evil or illness
anachronism	something out of place in time or history
analogy	partial likeness, similarity
anarchy	complete absence of government; lawlessness
animosity	ill will; strong dislike
annihilate	to demolish, destroy completely
annotation	explanatory note
annul	to cancel, do away with
anodyne	pain reliever
anomalous	abnormal, aberrant
anonymous	nameless; unknown person
antecedent	coming or happening before
anterior	preceding; previous; earlier

antipathetic	opposed; antagonistic
antipathy	aversion, deep-rooted dislike
antithesis	opposing or contrasting thoughts or ideas
apartheid	policy of racial segregation
apathetic	feeling little or no emotion, unmoved
aperture	opening, hole
aphorism	witty proverb or saying
aplomb	poise; self-possession
appease	to pacify or calm by giving in to demands; to acquiesce
apposite	appropriate, apt, well-suited
apprehensive	uneasy, wary, anxious
apprise	to notify, keep informed
approbation	official approval or sanction
apropos	pertinent, to the point
arbitrary	capricious; based on preference, notion, or whim
archaic	outdated; used only for special purposes or circumstances, as in rituals
archetype	prototype; the original pattern or model
armada	fleet of ships
arrogate	to appropriate; to claim or seize without right
artifice	guile, trickery, deceit
ascertain	to discover, find out without doubt
ascribe	to attribute to, point to as a cause
aseptic	bacteria-free; sterile
asperity	harshness, roughness

aspersion	disparaging remark or insinuation
assert	to declare, claim, state positively and firmly
assiduous	done with diligence and perseverance
astral	pertaining to the stars or heavens
ataxia	inability to control movement
attenuate	to dilute, weaken
atypical	unusual; not typical or characteristic
augment	to add to, increase
aural	pertaining to the ear or the sense of hearing
auspicious	promising good fortune or success; lucky
autocrat	domineering, self-willed person
avarice	greed
averse	reluctant, opposed to; unwilling
avert	to ward off or prevent from happening
avocation	hobby; something one does for pleasure and recreation
avuncular	like an uncle; mentoring

Drill 1

Choose the word or phrase that means most nearly the same as the *italicized* word.

1. affidavit
   a. postponed
   b. imported
   c. sworn statement
   d. denounced

2. accumulate
   a. gather
   b. compute
   c. thrown out
   d. release from prison

3. acquit
   a. walk out
   b. condemn
   c. set free
   d. apply for

4. adduce ·
   a. provide reasons
   b. compute
   c. suspect
   d. imply

5. adulation
   a. condemnation
   b. derision
   c. praise
   d. fretfulness

6. agoraphobia
   a. fear of spaces
   b. fear of cats
   c. fear of falling
   d. fear of heights

7. advocate
   a. speak to
   b. warn
   c. plead for
   d. scold

8. affirmation
   a. avowal
   b. familiarization
   c. denial
   d. strengthening

9. affluent
   a. high-speed
   b. well-spoken
   c. wealthy
   d. esoteric

10. aggregate
   a. sum
   b. irritate
   c. breach
   d. division

(1-c; 2-a; 3-c; 4-a; 5-c; 6-a; 7-c; 8-a; 9-c; 10-a)

Drill 2

Choose the word that best completes the meaning of the sentence.

1. The issue was put in _____ until all the data could be compiled.
   a. abhorrence   c. abatement
   b. abeyance   d. abrasion

2. The children became extremely _____ when they realized they were lost.
   a. aloof   c. affluent
   b. aesthetic   d. agitated

3. Keep me _____ of any changes in the patient's condition.
   a. apprised   c. asserted
   b. appeased   d. ascribed

4. She worked _____, staying late to make sure that the project was in order before the morning meeting.
   a. apathetically   c. auspiciously
   b. assiduously   d. autocratically

5. This particular incident is an _____; it has never happened before.
   a. altruism   c. archetype
   b. antipathy   d. anomaly

B

badinage	good-natured teasing; banter
banal	commonplace; trite
baneful	deadly; threatening; ruinous
bedlam	total confusion and disorder
beguile	to deceive or mislead by cheating or trickery
belie	to prove false
belittle	to criticize, diminish; to speak slightingly of
bellicose	quarrelsome, hostile; warlike
benign	not threatening or deadly; good-natured or kindly
berate	to scold, harangue, rebuke
bicameral	having two houses or official bodies, as in government
biennial	happening every two years
biped	two-footed animal
blatant	disagreeably obvious, loud, or noticeable
blithe	carefree; cheerful
bombastic	pompous; grandiloquent
bourgeois	middle-class; capitalistic
bovine	cow-like; slow and plodding
brazen	bold and shameless
brevity	conciseness, terseness
brusque	abrupt, curt
bucolic	rural; pertaining to the country life
buoyant	resilient; able to float
burgeon	to sprout or bloom
burnish	to polish, make shiny

Drill 3

Choose the word or phrase that means most nearly the same as the *italicized* word.

1. anodyne
   a. sleeping
   b. reddish
   c. pain reliever
   d. poisonous

2. baneful
   a. unhappy
   b. morose
   c. deadly
   d. obstreperous

3. beguile
   a. deceive
   b. wander
   c. fling
   d. harass

4. belie
   a. rest
   b. excuse
   c. prove false
   d. make appropriate

5. berate
   a. scold
   b. score
   c. confuse
   d. confute

6. biped
   a. two-wheeled
   b. side-swiped
   c. two-footed
   d. half-witted

7. blithe
   a. cheerful
   b. thin
   c. addle-brained
   d. stubborn

8. aseptic
   a. astringent
   b. rude
   c. bacteria-free
   d. cumulative

9. burgeon
   a. sprout
   b. bunion
   c. burnish
   d. bury

10. bourgeois
   a. boorish
   b. slow-cooked
   c. middle-class
   d. foreign-born

(1-c; 2-c; 3-a; 4-c; 5-a; 6-c; 7-a; 8-c; 9-a; 10-c)

C

cadaver	dead body
cadence	rhythm or flow of speech or movement
cajole	to coax, persuade pleasantly
callow	young, inexperienced; immature
calumniate	to slander
candor	impartial and fair statements; unprejudiced speech
capacious	roomy; spacious
capitol	central legislative building of a state or country
capitulate	to surrender conditionally
capricious	willfully erratic; flighty
captious	fault-finding, quibbling, hypercritical
carafe	bottle
carnage	slaughter, massacre
carnal	of the body or flesh; worldly, not spiritual
carnivorous	flesh-eating
castigate	to punish, criticize, rebuke severely
cataclysm	disaster or upheaval that causes sudden, violent change
caustic	burning; stinging
cavil	to quibble, find trivial objections
cede	to give over; to transfer ownership of something
celerity	speed, swiftness
cerebral	pertaining to the brain; highly intellectual

chagrin	frustration, disappointment
chary	wary, distrustful
chastise	to rebuke, condemn sharply
chattel	items of property
chide	to scold, reprove mildly
choleric	angry, argumentative
chronic	recurring; long-lasting
circuitous	roundabout; indirect
circumlocution	oblique, indirect, or lengthy way of saying something
circumspect	cautious in speech and action; careful to consider all aspects
circumvent	to get around or avoid something by planning or ingenuity
cite	to quote
clairvoyance	ability to perceive invisible or far-away things or events
clemency	mercy, leniency, as toward an offender or enemy
coalesce	to grow or come together
coalition	combination; union
coerce	to force, compel without permission or agreement
cogent	compelling; convincing, forceful
cogitate	to ponder, consider; to meditate
cognition	perception; the process of knowing and recognizing
cognizant	aware or informed of something

coherent	logically connected; consistent; clearly articulated
coincide	to correspond exactly; to come together at the same time
collaborate	to work together cooperatively
colloquial	conversational or informal speech
colloquy	formal discussion; conference
commensurate	equal in measure, size, or value
commodious	spacious, roomy
compel	to force or convince to do something
compensate	to provide equal payment for or make up for something else
complacent	self-satisfied, smug
complement	that which completes or brings to completion
compliant	yielding; agreeable
complicity	partnership in wrongdoing
comprehensible	intelligible; able to be understood
comprise	to include or consist of; to contain
compulsory	required; compelling
compunction	twinge of conscience; remorse
concede	to acknowledge or admit as true
concentric	sharing the same centerpoint
concept	abstract notion, idea, or thought
conciliate	to reconcile, bring together again
concise	brief; short and clear
concomitant	accompanying; attendant

concurrent	simultaneous, happening at the same time
condole	to express sympathy, commiserate
condone	to pardon, overlook, excuse
conducive	helping to make something happen
confiscate	to seize or appropriate, usually as a penalty
confute	to prove erroneous or false
congeal	to solidify or thicken by cooling or freezing
congruent	in agreement; corresponding
conjecture	inference, theory, or prediction based on guesswork
conjugal	pertaining to marriage
consanguineous	blood-related
conscientious	painstaking, diligent, precise, honest
consign	to hand over, entrust to
consonance	to be in accord, agreement, or harmony
constrain	to force or compel; to oblige
construe	to analyze; to interpret
contentious	quarrelsome, quick to argue
contiguous	adjacent, next to, adjoining
contingent	dependent on
contort	to twist or wrench out of shape
contract	formal agreement, usually written
contravene	to oppose, be in conflict with
contrive	to scheme, devise a plan
controversy	disputed subject; debate
contusion	bruise

convene	to gather together, assemble
converge	to approach, move nearer together
conversant	familiar, acquainted with; able to discuss knowledgeably
convivial	gay, festive, lively
convoke	to summon or call together a group
copious	plentiful; abundant
corpulent	stout; obese
corrigible	capable of being corrected, improved, or reformed
corroborate	to confirm with additional facts; to support
cosmopolitan	worldly, not provincial
countermand	to cancel or revoke an order
cower	to shrink back in fear
credence	belief or faith in the statements of another person
credible	reliable, worthy of being believed
credulous	easily convinced without much evidence, gullible
cryptic	mysterious; having a hidden meaning
culpable	at fault, blameworthy
cursory	superficial; hurried, hasty
curtail	to cut short, reduce

Drill 4

Choose the word or phrase that means most nearly the same as the *italicized* word.

1. *brazen*
   a. grilled
   b. quarrelsome
   c. tanned
   d. shameless

2. *contiguous*
   a. contingent
   b. cerebral
   c. celebration
   d. adjoining

3. *contravene*
   a. intercept
   b. interrupt
   c. approve
   d. oppose

4. *convene*
   a. help
   b. assemble
   c. monitor
   d. interpolate

5. *cavil*
   a. heat
   b. dance
   c. rot
   d. quibble

6. *corpulent*
   a. deceased
   b. obese
   c. flesh-eating
   d. circular

7. *complacent*
   a. composed
   b. adjoining
   c. surprised
   d. smug

8. *countermand*
   a. invoke
   b. revoke an order
   c. slap
   d. retired

9. *credence*
   a. harmony
   b. religion
   c. orthodoxy
   d. belief

10. *credulous*
    a. trustworthy
    b. gullible
    c. believable
    d. fatuous

(1-d; 2-d; 3-d; 4-b; 5-d; 6-b; 7-d; 8-b; 9-d; 10-b)

Drill 5

Choose the word that best completes the meaning of the sentence.

1. This _____ disregard for the rules will result in your dismissal!
   - a. baneful
   - b. blithe
   - c. blatant
   - d. bucolic

2. The train riders engaged in friendly _____ while the tracks were repaired.
   - a. badinage
   - b. bellicose
   - c. bombast
   - d. berating

3. They will certainly _____ if you offer them enough incentive to do so.
   - a. castigate
   - b. calumniate
   - c. cogitate
   - d. capitulate

4. Chronic tardiness is not _____ to job security.
   - a. concise
   - b. complacent
   - c. compliant
   - d. conducive

5. Federal agents were called in to _____ the counterfeit bills.
   - a. contingent
   - b. credible
   - c. confiscate
   - d. concur

(1-c; 2-a; 3-d; 4-d; 5-c)

2

Unlocking Meaning
The Components of English Words

The truly revolutionary technique to reaching the highest level of communication is learning the technique of "spinning off" — that is, learning the core meaning of English words, breaking them apart and rearranging them, attaching a visual memory key to each, and creating a richer, more powerful vocabulary. To do this, you will learn the meaning of the word components of English — prefixes, suffixes, and roots. It may remind you of your elementary school days, but this book uses a totally new method of capturing the significance of this simple approach. By using the visualizing techniques, you will come away with a deeper understanding of the English language.

Imagine an apple. It is composed of an outer layer of skin, a middle layer of flesh, and an inner core of seeds. By "peeling" away each layer, you discover what lies beneath. This simple analogy is what you will learn to do with words: you will "peel" away the prefixes, then the suffixes, to get to the core meaning of words.

Each section is blocked off into easily digestible sections. Interrelated word components are grouped together so that you can become more familiar with the "pieces" that will build synonyms and antonyms.

Work slowly in this part. The key to truly powerful communication skills is in recognizing these puzzle-pieces of English. You will learn how to visualize the essential meaning of the pieces. Later, when you are searching for the right word, you will step back and "describe" mentally exactly what you are observing — and reach for that visual key to construct the most precise word. For example, if you are describing something that is "twisted-out-of-shape," you will be able to reach for the visual key and say it in one word — "distorted."

PREFIXES

Prepositions: Group One

before, early, toward	**fore-**	forecast
	pre-	premature
	ante-	antedate
	pro-	proclaim
after, behind	**post-**	postpone

with, together	**col-**	collateral
	con-	concede
	cor-	correspond
	sym-	symphony
	syn-	synthesis
opposing, against	**anti-**	antihero
	contra-	contraband ·
	counter-	counterculture
	ob-	obfuscate
	with-	withhold

to, toward	**ad-**	adjacent
	at-	attribute
away, from	**ab-**	abnormal
	abs-	abstract
	apo-	apostasy

over, above	**hyper-**	hyperactive
	super-	supersonic
under, beneath, within	**hypo**	hypochondria
	sub-	subculture
	subter-	subterranean
	infra-	infrared

in, into, within	in-	inept
	im-	impart
	endo-	endometrium
	en-	envelope
	em-	embedded
out of, outside, beyond	ex-	expatriate
	exo-	exoskeleton
	ecto-	ectoplasm
	ef-	effluent
	e-	eliminate

Prepositions: Group Two

on, upon, beside	epi-	epidermis
between	inter-	interstate
beyond, extreme	extra-	extrasensory
	para-	paranormal
	meta-	metaphysical
	ultra-	ultraconservative
without, not	im-	immodest
	in-	indecent
	a-	atypical
	an-	anaerobic
far	tele-	telegraph
again, back	re-	return
back, backward	retro-	retrograde
aside	se-	sedition
behind, after	post-	postgraduate
around, about	circum-	circumference
	peri-	pericardium

down, from	**de-**	depress
	cata-	catastrophe
through, across, over	**dia-**	diagram
	per-	permeate
	pel-	pellucid
	trans-	transition

Quantifiers

much, many	**multi-**	multilevel
	poly-	polygamy
both, both sides	**ambi-**	ambidextrous
	amphi-	amphipod
several	**plu-**	plurality
equal	**equi-**	equivalent
	par-	parallel
half	**demi-**	demivolt
	hemi-	hemisphere
	semi-	semicircle
middle	**medi-**	medial
	meso-	mesolithic
enough	**sat-**	satiate
whole	**holo-**	hologram

all, every	**omni-**	omnipresent
	pan-	pantheism
not any, none	**null-**	nullification
	nihil-	nihilism
not, without, apart	**un-**	unnecessary

	non-	nonissue
	ig-	ignoble
	dis-	dishonest
	dif-	diffract

first, most	prim-	primeval
	primo-	primogenitor
	proto-	protozoan
	arch-	archenemy
last	ulti-	ultimately

one	uni-	unilateral
	mono-	monorail
	sol-	solipsism
two	du-	dual
	di-	dilemma
	bi-	bicameral
three	tri-	trinity
four	quad-	quadruple
	tetra-	tetraethyl
five	quint-	quintessence
	penta-	pentagram
six	sex-	sextant
	hexa-	hexagon
seven	sept-	September
	hepta-	heptagon
eight	octa-	octagenarian
	octo-	octopus
nine	non-	nonent
	nov-	novena

ten	**dec-**	decimal
hundred	**cent-**	centenary
	hect-	hectare
thousand	**mill-**	millimeter
	kilo-	kilohertz
one and a half	**sesqui-**	sesquipedalian

Drill 6

Choose the word component in the left-hand column that matches the meaning of the word element in the right-hand column.

1. per-	a. ultra-
2. with-	b. equi-
3. bi-	c. multi-
4. kilo-	d. circum-
5. par-	e. du-
6. arch-	f. syn-
7. poly-	g. mill-
8. extra-	h. dia-
9. con-	i. contra-
10. peri-	j. proto-

(1-h; 2-i; 3-e; 4-g; 5-b; 6-j; 7-c; 8-a; 9-f; 10-d)

SUFFIXES

Adjective and Adverb Endings

related, pertaining to	**-ary**	parliamentary
	-ory	contradictory
	-an	diocesan
causing	**-fic**	terrific
excessively, like	**-ose**	verbose

like, cabable of being	**-able**	lovable
	-ible	reversible
	-il	fossil
	-ile	juvenile
like, associated with	**-ine**	saturnine
	-ic	aristocratic
	-ical	angelical
	-ive	disruptive
	-ous	perilous
	-ac	monomaniac
	-al	maternal
resembling, tending to	**-some**	tiresome
	-like	godlike
	-ly	lovingly
	-ish	foolish
	-oid	anthropoid

Noun and Verb Endings:

Noun Endings

| practice or quality of | **-ism** | baptism |
| | **-ation** | affirmation |

	-ure	composure
	-tion	commotion
	-ment	enchantment
	-acy	celibacy
	-itude	verisimilitude
state or quality of	**-ry**	savagery
	-hood	parenthood
	-ship	friendship
	-ness	stubbornness
	-age	coverage
	-ity	stability
	-ance	vigilance
	-ence	despondence
one that does	**-er**	worker
	-ar	scholar
	-ary	functionary
	-or	orator
	-ent	superintendent
	-ant	accountant
	-ist	theorist
result, process	**-ment**	statement
	-sis	metamorphosis
rank or status	**-ian**	plebian

Verb Endings

to make	**-en**	quicken
	-ize	sanitize
	-ate	expatriate
	-fy	horrify

Drill 7

Choose the suffix in the right-hand column that matches the meaning of the suffix in the left-hand column

1. -able		a. -ical
2. -ous		b. -ish
3. -tion		c. -ist
4. -like		d. -ile
5. -ant		e. -itude

(1-d; 2-a; 3-e; 4-b; 5-c)

OTHER WORD COMPONENTS

Group One

large, great	**magni-**	magnify
	macro-	macrocosm
	maxi-	maxicoat
	mega-	megalopolis
small, miniature	**mini-**	minicomputer
	micro-	microprocessor

new	**neo-**	neolithic
	nov-	novel
old	**ger-**	gerontology
	paleo-	paleoanthropology
	vet-	veterinary
	sen-	senescent

good, well	**bene-**	benediction
	bon-	bonhomie
	eu-	eulogy
	well-	wellborn
wrong, bad	**mal-**	maladjustment
	mis-	misinformation

same, like	**homo-**	homogenous
	simul-	simulcast
other, another	**hetero-**	heterogamus
	ali-	alien
	alter-	alternator

true	**ver-**	veritable
false	**pseudo-**	pseudoscience
fast	**celer-**	celerity
slow	**tard-**	tardiness
brief, short	**brev-**	breviary
high	**acro-**	acrobat
	alti-	altitude
	alto-	altostratus
hard	**dur-**	durability
sharp	**ac-**	acidity
	acu-	acupuncture
mild, soft	**len-**	lenitive
	moll-	mollify
heavy	**grav-**	gravitation
worthy, strong	**val-**	value
	fort-	fortification
wise	**soph-**	sophistry
	sag-	sagacity
pleasing	**grat-**	gratify
hidden	**crypt-**	cryptogram
broad, wide	**lat-**	lateral
correct, straight	**rect-**	rectify
	ortho-	orthodox

Group Two

move	**mov-**	movability
	mob-	mobile
	mot-	motive
	kine-	kinematics
move forward, step	**grad-**	gradient
	-gress-	regressive

slope, bend	**-clin-**	declination
	-clino-	inclinometer
	-cliv-	declivity
climb	**-scend**	ascend
tend toward, cling	**-ver-**	convergence
	-her-	coherent
	hes-	hesitate

twist	**-tort-**	distorted
turn	**-vert-**	invert
	-stroph-	antistrophe
	rot-	rotary
bend	**-flec-**	inflection

tear apart, break	**rupt-**	rupture
	frac-	fraction
	frag-	fragmentary
fall	**cad-**	cadenza
	-cid-	incident
roll, turn	**-volv-**	evolve
	-volut-	convoluted

weigh, hang	**pend-**	pendulum
stir up, spin	**turb-**	turbid
	gyr-	gyration
	gyro-	gyroscope
flow	**flu-**	fluid
	fluv-	fluvial
stretch	**ten-**	tension
bring, carry, bear	**-fer-**	conifer
	port-	porter
stand	**sta-**	stable
	stat-	statue
place, put	**-pon-**	postponement
	-posit-	preposition
sit	**sed-**	sedate
	sess-	session

Drill 8

Choose the word component in the right-hand column that matches the meaning of the word element in the left-hand column.

1. bene-	a. mega-
2. macro-	b. alti-
3. neo-	c. gyr-
4. acro-	d. eu-
5. -turb	e. nov-

(1-d; 2-a; 3-e; 4-b; 5-c)

Group Three

pour, melt	**-fus-**	confusion
cleanse	**purg-**	purgatory
cut	**-sect**	dissect
cut, kill	**-cide**	genocide
	-cis-	decision
harm, injure	**noc-**	nocent
measure	**-meter**	odometer
	-mens-	dimension
manage	**-nomy**	agronomy
mark	**stig-**	stigmata
owe	**deb-**	debenture
lie	**-cumb-**	incumbent
send	**-mit**	submit
	mis-	missive
shut, close	**claus-**	claustrophobic
	clos-	closure
	-clud-	exclude
	-clus-	seclusion
clap	**-plode**	implode
throw, do	**jac-**	jactitation
	-jec-	injection
hold	**ten-**	tenable
	-tain	maintain
hold in	**-hibit**	exhibit

fill	**-com-**	incomplete
empty	**vac-**	vacancy

draw, pull	**tract-**	tractable
push, drive, beat	**-pel**	repel
	puls-	pulsate

join	**junct-**	junction
separate	**cess-**	cessation

loosen	**solv-**	solvent
	solu-	soluble
free	**lib-**	liberty
bind	**string-**	stringent
	-strict-	restriction

go	**-ced-**	procedure
come	**-ven-**	convene
	-vent	advent

take	**cap-**	captive
	-cept-	receptacle
give, endow	**dat-**	dated
	don-	donate
	dot-	doting

Group Four

life	**viv-**	vivid
	vit-	vital

	zoo-	zoology
	bio-	biosphere
breath, life	spir-	spirit
death	mori-	moribund
	mort-	mortality
	thana-	thanatopsis

body, flesh	carn-	carnal
	corp-	corporeal
	soma-	somatology
skin	derm-	dermatogen
	cut-	cutin
head	-cap-	decapitate
foot	ped-	pedometer
	pod-	podium
hand	manu-	manual
	chiro-	chiropody

origin, birth	gen-	genetic
born, produced	nat-	nature
end	fin-	finite
	termin-	terminal
sleep	dorm-	dormant
	somn-	somnolent
	sopor-	soporific
	hypno-	hypnosis
	morph-	morphology
	coma-	comatose

Group Five

time	**-chron-**	synchronize
	tempor-	temporary
time, age	**-ev-**	medieval

star	**aster-**	asterisk
	astro-	astronaut
	stell-	stellar
world, universe	**cosmo-**	cosmopolitan
place	**loc-**	location
	top-	topography
	stead-	steadfast
earth	**geo-**	geography
	terr-	territory

| wind | **vent-** | ventilation |

day	**diu-**	diurnal
	dia-	diarist
	jour-	journal
year	**-ann-**	biannual
night	**noct-**	nocturne

cold, freezing	**cryo-**	cryogenics
heat	**therm-**	thermal
fire	**flam-**	flammatory
	pyro-	pyromaniac
	ign-	ignition
burn	**caust-**	caustic

water	**aqua-**	aquaculture
	hydro-	hydrofoil
sea	**mar-**	marina
moon	**lun-**	lunatic
	mon-	monthly
sun	**sol-**	solarium
	helio-	heliotrophe
light	**lum-**	luminary
	luc-	lucidity
	photo-	photosynthesis
ray	**radi-**	radium
shadow	**umbr-**	umbrage

Group Six

man	**anthro-**	anthropomorphic
	homo-	homage
	vir-	virility
woman	**gyn-**	gynecology
child	**ped-**	pediatrician
	pedo-	pedology

father	**pater-**	paternal
mother	**mater-**	maternity
brother	**frater-**	fraternal
sister	**soror-**	sorority

friend	**ami-**	amiable
I	**ego-**	egoist
self	**auto-**	autocrat
	sui-	suicidal
name	**nom-**	nominal
	-onym	synonym

Group Seven

holy, sacred	**sacr-**	sacrifice
	sanct-	sanctuary
	hier-	hierophant
god	**dei-**	deity
	theo-	theocracy
sin	**-pecc-**	impeccable
healing	**-iatr-**	podiatry
faith	**fid-**	fiduciary
	tru-	trustee
mind, spirit	**psych-**	psychology
	-noia	paranoia
spirit	**anima-**	animation

circle	**-orb-**	suborbit
	-cycl-	unicycle
ship	**nau-**	nautilus
stone	**petro-**	petroglyph
	lith-	lithoid

carving	**glyph-**	glyphography
	sculp-	sculpture
money, gain	**pecun-**	pecuniary
	lucr-	lucre
road	**via-**	viacom
wall	**-mur-**	immured

Group Eight

believe	**-cred-**	incredible
opinion	**-dox**	heterodox
consider, reckon	**puta-**	putative
wish	**vol-**	volunteer
think, know, sense	**-sci-**	pseudoscience
	sens-	sensate
	sent-	sentimental
	wit-	wittingly
	gnos-	gnostic
hope	**-sper-**	desperado

government by, rule	**-cracy**	plutocracy
crowd	**greg-**	gregarious
rule	**dom-**	dominion
ruler, leader	**-gogue**	demagogue
people	**demo-**	democratic
	pop-	population
peace	**pac-**	pacify

war	**belli-**	belligerent
conquer	**vinc-**	vincibility
	vict-	victory
	vanqu-	vanquish
lead	**-duc-**	deduct
city	**-polit-**	apolitical
	-polis	Heliopolis
	civ-	civility
struggle	**agon-**	agonize
power	**dynam-**	dynamo

Group Nine

praise, glory	**laud-**	laudable
cry out	**-clam-**	proclamation
	-plor-	implore
deceive	**fal-**	falsification
blame	**culp-**	culpable
deny	**-neg-**	abnegate
take an oath, swear	**jur-**	jury
jest	**joc-**	jocularity
play, game	**lud-**	ludic
speak, talk, say	**dic-**	dictator
	loqu-	loquacity
	-loc-	elocution
	-voc-	convocation
	-cit-	recitative

laugh	**ris-**	risible
	rid-	ridiculous
ask, inquire, seek	**peti-**	petitioner
	-quis-	inquisitory
	quer-	query
	rog-	rogation
warn, remind	**-mon-**	admonish

Drill 9

Match each word in the left-hand column with its definition in the right-hand column.

1. centennial
2. prospective
3. circumspect
4. multinational
5. clamorous
6. antebellum
7. contrary
8. impassioned
9. obdurate
10. nominal

a. before the war
b. going against
c. in name only
d. hard, unyielding
e. looking forward
f. careful; looking in all directions
g. hundred-year anniversary
h. in many countries
i. full of strong feelings
j. shouting

(1-g; 2-e; 3-f; 4-h; 5-j; 6-a; 7-b; 8-i; 9-d; 10-c)

Group Ten

teach	**doc-**	doctrine
	tut-	tutorial
	-tui-	intuitive
learn	**cogn-**	cognition

science, theory	**-logy**	theology

remember	**mne-**	mnemonic
forget	**obliv-**	oblivion
writing	**-scrip-**	inscription
	graph-	graphic
	gram-	grammar
	scrib-	scribble
word	**verb-**	verbal
read, choose	**lect-**	lecture
	leg-	legible
book	**lib-**	librarian
	biblio-	bibliophile

Drill 10

Find the word on the right that contains a word component that means the same as the word(s) in the left column.

1.	money	a.	permutation
2.	game	b.	mariner
3.	sea	c.	ludicrous
4.	middle	d.	mediator
5.	to change	e.	lucrative
6.	to remember	f.	scripture
7.	to choose	g.	amnesty
8.	to teach	h.	proverb
9.	writing	i.	elect
10.	word	j.	indoctrinate

(1-e; 2-c; 3-b; 4-d; 5-a; 6-g; 7-i; 8-j; 9-f; 10-h)

Group Eleven

see, observe	**spec-**	spectator
	-scop-	periscope
	scrut-	scrutiny
	vid-	videodisc
	vis-	vision
touch, feel	**-tang-**	intangible
	tact-	tactile
feel, sense	**(a)esthe-**	an(a)esthesia
hearing, sound	**son-**	sonic
	phono-	phonograph
	aud-	audible
	acou-	acoustics
silence	**tac-**	taciturn
eat	**vor-**	voracity
gnaw	**rod-**	rodent

care	**-cur-**	security
heart	**cord-**	cordial
	card-	cardiologist
feelings, suffering	**path-**	pathos
	-pass-	impassioned
love	**-amor-**	inamorata
	phil-	philanthropist
fear	**-phobia**	xenophobia

Drill 11

Match each word on the left with its definition in the right-hand column.

1.	recede	a.	state as the truth
2.	abdicate	b.	throw light on
3.	homogenize	c.	give up a power
4.	illuminate	d.	put into words
5.	supervise	e.	go away
6.	verbalize	f.	oversee
7.	legislate	g.	make laws
8.	intervene	h.	draw out
9.	aver	i.	make the same through-
10.	protract		out
		j.	come between

(1-e; 2-c; 3-i; 4-b; 5-f; 6-d; 7-g; 8-j; 9-a; 10-h)

Group Twelve

walk	**ambu-**	ambulatory
	-patet-	peripatetic
run	**curr-**	current
	curs-	cursory
flee	**fug-**	fugitive
follow	**sequ-**	sequel
	-sec-	consecutively
travel, wander	**err-**	errant
	-migr-	immigrant
leap, jump	**-sault**	assault
	-sult-	desultory
	-sil-	resiliency
	sal-	sally

form, shape	**morph-**	morpheme
skill, craft, art	**techno-**	technological
build	**-struct-**	destruction
grow	**-cre-**	incremental
multiply, increase	**aug-**	augmentation
change	**mut-**	mutate
shape	**form-**	formation
use	**-sum-**	consumer
make, do	**ag-**	agency
	act-	react

	fac-	facilitate
	fic-	fiction
work, toil	**labor-**	laboratory
	-oper-	inoperable

Drill 12

Match each word on the left with its definition in the right-hand column.

1. mutable	a. able to be touched
2. culpable	b. laughable
3. interminable	c. ancient
4. amiable	d. holding firmly
5. vital	e. necessary to life
6. primeval	f. unending
7. tenacious	g. unable to be loosened
8. tangible	h. changeable
9. risible	i. friendly
10. indissoluble	j. blameworthy

(1-h; 2-j; 3-f; 4-i; 5-e; 6-c; 7-d; 8-a; 9-b; 10-g)

Drill 13

Find the word on the right that contains a word component that means the same as the word(s) in the left column.

1. on	a. ingratitude
2. to deceive	b. epitaph
3. son	c. fraternize
4. to bend	d. gravitate
5. to shape	e. refuge
6. brother	f. deflect
7. to flee	g. infallible
8. origin, birth	h. generate
9. pleasing	i. conformity
10. heavy	j. affiliate

(1-b; 2-g; 3-j; 4-f; 5-i; 6-c; 7-e; 8-h; 9-a; 10-d)

ESSENTIAL VOCABULARY II

D

dappled	spotted
dearth	lack of, scarcity; famine
debase	to cheapen, make lower in value
debauch	to corrupt, lead astray
debilitate	to weaken; to enervate
deceive	to trick, betray
deciduous	shedding leaves
decimate	to destroy or kill a large portion or part of something
decorous	proper; according to formal custom
deduce	to infer by logical reasoning from known facts or general principles
deduct	to subtract, take away
deference	respectful or courteous regard
defile	to profane or sully; to make unclean
defoliate	to strip of leaves
defunct	dead or extinct
degenerate	to have deteriorated or regressed
deify	to make into or treat as a god
delete	to cross out; to omit
deleterious	injurious; harmful to health or well-being
delineate	to trace or sketch the outline of something
demean	to degrade, debase
demote	to lower in status or position
demur	to hesitate; to object because of doubts

demure   coy; affectedly modest or shy

denigrate   to defame or disparage someone or something's worth or character

denizen   dweller, inhabitant

deplete   to empty; to take away reserves

deplore   to lament, regret

deprecate   to belittle, depreciate

depredation   plunder

deride   to ridicule, laugh at in contempt or scorn

derogatory   critical, negative, disparaging

desecrate   to dishonor or abuse something sacred; to make profane

designate   to appoint, name for an office or duty

destitute   living in complete poverty; wretched

desultory   lacking direction or purpose; random

deterrent   something that prevents or turns away something else

detract   to take away from; to deflect

deviate   to turn aside from a given course

devious   crooked or roundabout; untrustworthy

devise   to work out a plan; to invent

dictum   a pronouncement or formal statement of fact

didactic   used or intended for teaching or instruction

diffidence   lack of self-confidence; hesitancy; shyness

diffuse   to spread out, disperse

digress   to ramble, depart from the main subject

dilate   to become wider or larger

dilatory   inclined to delay; slow or late in doing things

dilemma	situation in which one must choose between unpleasant alternatives
discernible	able to be perceived or recognized
disclaim	to give up or renounce any claim to or connection with
disconcert	to embarrass or upset someone's composure
discordant	causing disharmony, dissonant
discreet	circumspect; careful about what one says or does; prudent
discrete	separate and distinct; unattached
discursive	rambling; desultory; digressive
disinterested	impartial; unbiased
disparage	to belittle, disdain
disparity	inequality or difference in rank, amount, or quality
dispel	to disperse, scatter
disquieting	restless; uneasy; disturbing
dissemble	to pretend, simulate, feign
disseminate	to scatter, spread abroad, promulgate
dissension	difference of opinion, disagreement
dissolute	debauched and dissipated; profligate
dissonant	opposing; incompatible
dissuade	to advise against something
distraught	crazed; mad with emotion such as grief
diurnal	daily
diverge	to go or move in different directions from a common point, branch off
divest	to strip or take away

divisive	causing disagreement or dissension
divulge	to reveal, make public
docile	compliant, easily taught or led
dogmatic	stating opinion in an arrogant, pompous manner
doldrums	state of listlessness, dullness
dormant	sleeping or at rest
dossier	file of information kept on someone or something
droll	amusing
dubious	doubtful; ambiguous, vague
duplicity	hypocritical cunning or deception; double-dealing

Drill 14

Choose the word or phrase·that means most nearly the same as the *italicized* word.

1. cryptic
   a. embalmed
   b. dried-out
   c. ancient
   d. mysterious

2. divergent
   a. simultaneous
   b. differing
   c. approaching
   d. parallel

3. conceded
   a. denied
   b. explained
   c. implied
   d. admitted

4. cognizant
   a. rare
   b. reluctant
   c. aware
   d. haphazard

5. corroboration
   a. expenditure
   b. compilation
   c. confirmation
   d. reduction

6. defoliate
   a. infect
   b. strip of leaves
   c. unravel
   d. unearth

7. desultory
   a. errant
   b. dejected
   c. aimless
   d. destitute

8. dilatory
   a. slow
   b. enlarged
   c. aimless
   d. expansive

9. congruent
   a. noisy
   b. agreeing
   c. quarrelsome
   d. sticky

10. denizen
   a. cellar
   b. confusion
   c. sorcerer
   d. dweller

(1-d; 2-b; 3-d; 4-c; 5-c; 6-b; 7-c; 8-a; 9-b; 10-d)

Drill 15

Choose the word that best completes the meaning of the sentence.

1. Spruce and hemlock are coniferous, not _____, trees.
   a. debauch   c. defoliation
   b. deciduous   d. desecration

2. Your _____ will be misinterpreted as lack of interest.
   a. diffidence   c. deprecation
   b. deference   d. deviation

3. Please keep these two groups _____; they are not to be confused or combined.
   a. discreet   c. docile
   b. discordant   d. discrete

4. You shouldn't _____ those less fortunate than yourself.
   a. disparage   c. divulge
   b. dissemble   d. digress

5. _____ yourself of unnecessary expenditures and your budget will balance.
   a. Divulge   c. Diverge
   b. Divest   d. Dissuade

(1-b; 2-a; 3-d; 4-a; 5-b)

E

eclectic	collected from various sources
ecology	science of the relationship between living organisms and their environment
ecstasy	state of overpowering emotion such as joy
edify	to enlighten, instruct
effect	(*v.*) to bring about; (*n.*) result
efficacious	producing the desired effect; effective
effrontery	audacity, brazenness; boldness
effusive	overflowing, copious
egocentric	self-centered
egotism	constant, excessive reference to oneself
egress	exit, way out
elated	extremely happy
elicit	to bring out, evoke
elucidate	to clarify, explain
elude	to evade, escape
elusive	baffling; hard to grasp mentally
emetic	substance used to induce vomiting
enact	to decree, ordain
encroach	to creep up; to invade or infringe upon
enervate	to debilitate, weaken
engender	to beget, bring into being
engross	to absorb the entire attention of someone
engulf	to overwhelm, swallow up
enigma	puzzle, inexplicable situation
enlighten	to reveal truths to, edify
enmity	bitter hostility, antagonism

ensnare	to trap or trick into being caught
ensue	to follow immediately afterward
enunciate	to speak or pronounce clearly
ephemeral	transitory, fleeting, short-lived
epicure	one who enjoys excellent food and drink
epithet	descriptive nickname or title
equanimity	composure, calmness, even-temperedness
equivocal	purposely vague, misleading, or ambiguous
erode	to eat away at something; to cause to disintegrate
ersatz	imitation; substitution
erudite	scholarly, learned, showing wide knowledge
eschew	to shun, avoid
esoteric	information or concepts meant to be understood by only a chosen few
ethereal	heavenly, celestial
ethical	conforming to the standards of conduct and performance of a given profession or group
etiology	study of causes, sources, or beginnings
eulogy	speech or writing praising the deceased
euphemism	polite or inoffensive way of saying something unpleasant
euphoria	extreme feeling of well-being or happiness
euthanasia	mercy killing, induced painless death
evasion	subterfuge; avoidance
evince	to indicate or show clearly

evolution	gradual change and development
exacerbate	to exasperate; to continually annoy
excoriate	to denounce harshly; to flay or strip skin off something
execrable	totally inferior, of the lowest or poorest quality
execrate	to loathe, abhor, detest
exempt	to excuse or free from a rule or obligation
exhort	to urge on, strongly encourage
exonerate	to prove not guilty, exculpate
exorbitant	excessive, beyond what is reasonable or appropriate
expedient	advantageous, convenient for achieving a desired result
expertise	specialized skill, knowledge, or judgment
exigency	urgent necessity
expiate	to pay the penalty for wrongdoing
explicate	to explain comprehensively and in detail
expurgate	to edit out sections considered obscene or objectionable
extemporaneous	presenting information without any preparation
extenuate	to lessen or mitigate by providing excuses or explanations
extirpate	to exterminate, abolish, remove completely
extricate	to free or release from an entanglement
extrinsic	from outside, external
extrude	to push or force out

Drill 16

Choose the word or phrase that is most **opposite** in meaning to the *italicized* word.

1. *encroach*
   a. reclined
   b. infest with
   c. retreat
   d. crusted

2. *effrontery*
   a. bombast
   b. falsified
   c. beribboned
   d. shyness

3. *cursory*
   a. thorough
   b. impolite
   c. honest
   d. quickly

4. *ersatz*
   a. imported
   b. tainted
   c. melodramatic
   d. genuine

5. *debilitate*
   a. encourage
   b. insinuate
   c. prepare
   d. strengthen

6. *eclectic*
   a. brilliant
   b. exclusive
   c. pastoral poem
   d. conclusive

7. *deride*
   a. fly
   b. praise
   c. amend
   d. admit

8. *discern*
   a. misperceive
   b. emit
   c. expand
   d. deploy

9. *discrete*
   a. prudent
   b. joined
   c. crooked
   d. stunted

10. *dissonance*
   a. disapproval
   b. disaster
   c. harmony
   d. disparity

(1-c; 2-d; 3-a; 4-d; 5-d; 6-b; 7-b; 8-a; 9-b; 10-c)

Drill 17

Choose the word that best completes the meaning of the sentence.

1. Please don't speak so rapidly; if you don't _____ clearly, the students won't understand.
   a. elucidate
   b. enervate
   c. enunciate
   d. edify

2. You will _____ distrust if you don't reveal all of the information at the beginning.
   a. engender
   b. erode
   c. ensue
   d. eschew

3. The answer he gave was an _____. No one could figure out its true meaning.
   a. enmity
   b. epicure
   c. esoteric
   d. enigma

4. Given the _____ circumstances, we will not charge you a late fee.
   a. extenuating
   b. exonerated
   c. exacerbating
   d. euphoric

5. Choose the most _____ method you can — time is precious!
   a. exorbitant
   b. expedient
   c. excoriated
   d. execrable

(1-c; 2-a; 3-d; 4-a; 5-b)

Drill 18

Choose the word or phrase that means most nearly the same as the *italicized* word.

1. *droll*
   a. short
   b. drunken
   c. amusing
   d. rotund

2. *deprecate*
   a. lower the worth
   b. express disapproval
   c. apologize for
   d. applaud

3. *culpable*
   a. dangerous
   b. soft
   c. blameworthy
   d. easily perceived

4. *coherent*
   a. not clear
   b. courteous
   c. specific
   d. logically related

5. *doldrums*
   a. rumbling
   b. arcane
   c. darkened
   d. dullness

(1-c; 2-b; 3-c; 4-d; 5-d)

3

Spinning Off
Increasing Your
Functional Vocabulary

CHANGING WORD COMPONENTS

The possibilities for increasing the size of your functional vocabulary are almost endless once you understand the simple principle of spinning off the word components of English — changing prefixes and suffixes to change meaning and parts of speech. A well-kept secret of vocabulary building is not just learning a lot of new words, but learning how to use the words you know in many different ways, simply by changing a piece of it here and there.

Let's create an easy diagram, using the simple word component "gress" as our spin-off core. Its basic visual key is "to move forward," as you learned on page 36.

With an assortment of prefixes spoking out to the left and suffixes to the right, you begin to understand the "spinning-off" image. Add a prefix "re" and a suffix "ion" and you create a

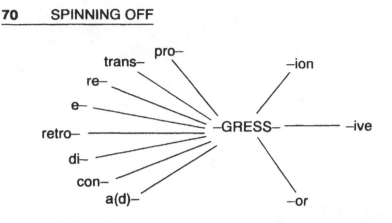

noun with the visual meaning of "the act or quality of moving back." Change the puzzle pieces to add "pro" and "ive" and you create an adjective meaning "moving-ahead-like." Switch again with "a" and "or" and you've fashioned a noun meaning "one who moves toward." Try "con" + "gress" + "ion" and add another suffix, "al," to create "congressional."

Now try using the spinning-off technique to create synonyms, words with similar meaning. This time let's use the word component "lib," which means "to free." Fix that visual image in your mind as you quickly spin off as many words as you can think of containing that puzzle piece: liberty, liberate, liberation, ad lib, deliberate, and so forth.

Now remember that when you first learned that puzzle piece, it was grouped with another one with a similar meaning—"solv" or "solu," meaning "to loosen" (on page 40). If you "free" something, you've "let it loose." Use memory keys such as this to help you keep related puzzle pieces in your mind. Try spinning off quickly on these new pieces: solve, solution, absolve, solvent, absolution, insoluble, and so forth. Can you see the "visual" common denominator in these words? It's the image of "loosening" something that had been hidden or tightly bound up: a solvent loosens a stubborn stain; a solution to a mystery "frees up" the answer.

You can also use this technique to learn opposite meanings—antonyms. The opposite meaning of loosen or free is to tighten or bind, and thereby the word components "string" or "strict" (on page 40). Immediately you see that "string" in its most basic sense of being used to tie something up! Spin off: stringent, astringent, strict, restrict, constriction. An astringent is used to tighten the pores on your skin, and we all know what a boa constrictor does to its victims!

There are no specific drills on this technique because there are as many "answers" to spinning off as you yourself can create. Whenever you learn a new word component or word from the vocabulary lists in this book, pull the word apart to find its core puzzle pieces—and spin off in your head new words, new parts of speech, related words, and opposite words as you go through your day. You will instantly bring whole lists of words into your recognition vocabulary!

Drill 19

Match each word on the right with its definition in the left-hand column.

1. state as the truth		a. recede
2. throw light on		b. abdicate
3. give up a power		c. homogenize
4. put into words		d. illuminate
5. go away		e. supervise
6. oversee		f. verbalize
7. make laws		g. legislate
8. draw out		h. intervene
9. make the same throughout	i. aver
10. come between		j. protract

(1-i; 2-d; 3-b; 4-f; 5-a; 6-e; 7-g; 8-j; 9-c; 10-h)

Drill 20

Divide the word on the left into word components, and then find the word in the right-hand column that means the same as one of those components.

1. nominee	a. none, nothing
2. annihilate	b. night
3. oblivious	c. name
4. impending	d. to manage
5. repatriate	e. to forget
6. impecunious	f. peace
7. nocturnal	g. father
8. impeccable	h. sin
9. pacify	i. money
10. autonomy	j. to hang, weigh

(1-c; 2-a; 3-e; 4-j; 5-g; 6-i; 7-b; 8-h; 9-f; 10-d)

Drill 21

Choose the word component in the left-hand column that is **opposite** in meaning from the word component in the right-hand column.

1.	therm-	a.	lun-
2.	clam-	b.	laud-
3.	belli-	c.	ambu-
4.	obliv-	d.	dia-
5.	tact-	e.	tac-
6.	culp-	f.	cryo-
7.	helio-	g.	tut-
8.	curs-	h.	mne-
9.	noct-	i.	pac-
10.	cogn-	j.	son-

(1-f; 2-e; 3-i; 4-h; 5-j; 6-b; 7-a; 8-c; 9-d; 10-g)

ESSENTIAL VOCABULARY III

F

facade	front of a building; false front or disguise
facile	working or done easily; fluent; adept
facilitate	to make easier; to remove obstacles or delays
fallacious	false, misleading, deceptive
fallible	capable of error or misjudgment
fastidious	fussy, squeamish; particular to a fault
fatuous	inane; silly; foolish
feasible	capable of being done, possible
feckless	weak, ineffective, irresponsible
fiasco	embarrassing failure
finite	having measurable or definable limits
fiscal	pertaining to finances
flammable	capable of being ignited
flaunt	to display conspicuously, impudently, or defiantly
flout	to disregard, scoff at, or be scornful of something
fluctuate	to vary, be continually changing
foray	raid; plunder
frenetic	frenzied, harried
futile	useless, pointless, without result

G

garish	gaudy, overdone; in poor taste
garrulous	loquacious; annoyingly chatty

gauche	tactless; lacking social grace
generic	generalized; common to or of a group or class
genial	cheerful, friendly, amiable
geriatrics	branch of medicine dealing with the diseases and conditions of old age
germane	pertinent, relevant, to the point
gist	essential meaning
goad	to challenge, prod, push
gratuitous	free, given without payment; additional; unearned
gratuity	tip; gift of money for a service rendered
gregarious	sociable, fond of the company of others
guile	deceit, cunning
gyrate	to turn, whirl, spin

H

halcyon	calm, peaceful, undisturbed
harass	to annoy or intrude repeatedly
heinous	unspeakably abominable; outrageously wicked
helix	spiral, coil
heterodox	unorthodox, iconoclastic; departing from the status quo
heterogeneous	from a different origin or source
hindsight	wisdom after-the-fact; realizing after an event what should have been done
hirsute	covered with hair
histrionic	melodramatic, overly emotional

holocaust	total destruction by fire
homicide	killing of one person by another
homogeneous	similar or identical; from the same source or origin
hyperbole	exaggeration for literary or oratorical effect
hypochondria	excessive worry and complaining about one's health
hypothesis	unproved theory or proposition

Drill 22

Choose the word or phrase that means most nearly the same as the *italicized* word.

1. *fiasco*
   a. lively
   b. quick-witted
   c. broiled
   d. failure

2. *fatuous*
   a. obnoxiously foolish
   b. excessively generous
   c. obese
   d. gaseous

3. *flammable*
   a. fireproof
   b. kiln-dried
   c. capable of being ignited
   d. igneous

4. *foray*
   a. attempt
   b. swinging
   c. porch
   d. plunder

5. *generic*
   a. communicable
   b. esoteric
   c. pertaining to race or kind
   d. variegated

6. *gratuitous*
   a. thankful
   b. inexpensive
   c. dubious
   d. free

7. *heinous*
   a. ridiculous
   b. atrocious
   c. of the blood
   d. somber

8. *guile*
   a. woven
   b. hammered
   c. emblazon
   d. deceit

9. *heterodox*
   a. paradoxical
   b. nonconforming
   c. dilemma
   d. imperturbable

10. *hindsight*
   a. prescience
   b. overseeing
   c. foreboding
   d. looking backward

(1-d; 2-a; 3-c; 4-d; 5-c; 6-d; 7-b; 8-d; 9-b; 10-d)

Drill 23

Choose the word or phrase that is most **opposite** in meaning to the *italicized* word.

1. *decorous*
   a. improper
   b. superficial
   c. removable
   d. inappropriate

2. *conversant*
   a. terse
   b. pushy
   c. convinced
   d. unfamiliar

3. *dappled*
   a. sampled
   b. ruined
   c. ignored
   d. unspotted

4. *derogatory*
   a. uneven
   b. equal
   c. opposite
   d. flattering

5. *depredation*
   a. plethora
   b. gross
   c. restoration
   d. glamour

(1-a; 2-d; 3-d; 4-d; 5-c)

Drill 24

Match each word on the right with its definition in the left-hand column.

1. wrong name	a. dislocation
2. withdrawal	b. misanthropy
3. knowing in advance	c. misnomer
4. denial	d. negation
5. power of will	e. propulsion
6. forerunner	f. volition
7. putting out of place	g. retraction
8. pushing forward	h. inclination
9. hatred of mankind	i. precognition
10. leaning toward	j. precursor

(1-c; 2-g; 3-i; 4-d; 5-f; 6-j; 7-a; 8-e; 9-b; 10-h)

I

iconoclast	one who flouts or criticizes beliefs as outmoded or superstitious
ideology	values, doctrines, or set opinions of a person or specific group
idiosyncrasy	peculiarities, eccentricities
ignoble	dishonorable; mean
ignominious	disgraceful; discrediting
illegible	difficult or impossible to read due to the poor quality of printing or writing
illicit	forbidden; not allowed by law or custom
illuminate	to clarify, give the meaning of; to light up
illusory	fleeting, dreamlike, elusive
impalpable	not capable of being detected or perceived
impassioned	filled with emotion, fiery
impeccable	faultless, flawless
impecunious	penniless, poor
impede	to obstruct, cause delay
impel	to push into motion, drive forward
imperative	urgent, compelling
imperturbable	unflappable, not easily upset or excited
impervious	incapable of being penetrated or breached
impetuous	rash, impulsive
imponderable	unable to be comprehended or measured
importune	to beg; to demand
imprecation	curse
impugn	to cast doubt on someone's character or truthfulness

impunity	freedom from punishment
impute	to attribute to, ascribe
inadvertent	done in oversight or by mistake, unintentional
inalienable	permanent; cannot be taken away
inception	beginning, start, commencement
incessant	endless, unceasing
incognito	disguised; unrecognized
incorrigible	incapable of being corrected, improved, or reformed
inculcate	to indoctrinate; to impress by frequent repetition
indict	to formally charge with a crime
indolent	idle; lazy
indubitable	unquestionable; without doubt
induct	to formally lead or bring into
indurate	hardened; callous or unfeeling
inept	bungling; inefficient; gauche
inexorable	unrelenting, immovable
infraction	minor breaking of a law or rule
ingenuous	guileless; open; candid, frank
ingratiate	to intentionally gain someone's favor or indebtedness
inherent	inborn, innate
inhibition	unconscious psychological process that suppresses an action, emotion, or thought
innocuous	harmless
inquisitive	curious, inclined to ask questions, eager to learn

insatiable	constantly wanting more, unsatisfiable; greedy
inscrutable	obscure; mysterious, enigmatic
insolvent	bankrupt
instigate	to stir up trouble or disagreement
insubordinate	defiant and disobedient
intangible	not able to be touched, defined, or reached
integral	essential, necessary for completeness
integration	unification, bringing together all parts into a whole
intercede	to plead for or make a request on behalf of another
intercept	to head off, prevent; to hinder
interpolate	to change by adding new words or subject matter
interregnum	interval between the reigns of two successive sovereigns
intractable	unruly, stubborn; difficult to manage
intransigent	uncompromising; refusing to come to an agreement or be reconciled
intrepid	bold, dauntless; fearless
intrinsic	essential, inherent
introvert	introspective, inward-looking
inundate	to flood or overflow
inveigh	to argue vehemently
inverse	directly opposite
invidious	eliciting ill will, jealousy, or envy
irony	humorous form of sarcasm in which the intended meaning of the words used is the opposite of their usual meaning

irreconcilable   ideas that cannot be brought into harmony or agreement

irritate   to rub the wrong way, annoy

iterate   to repeat, do over and over

itinerant   traveling from place to place

Drill 25

Choose the word or phrase that means most nearly the same as the *italicized* word.

1. *frenetic*
   a. obsolete
   b. curled
   c. obtuse
   d. frenzied

2. *bedlam*
   a. serenity
   b. dormitory
   c. salve
   d. confusion

3. *ignominious*
   a. flammable
   b. disgraceful
   c. unschooled
   d. highly explosive

4. *illicit*
   a. draw out
   b. barely perceivable
   c. not necessary
   d. not licensed

5. *impeccable*
   a. persnickety
   b. faultless
   c. painstaking
   d. unadulterated

6. *impediment*
   a. cavity
   b. aperture
   c. luggage
   d. obstacle

7. *chary*
   a. burned
   b. cautious
   c. frustrated
   d. twisted

8. *impervious*
   a. accepting
   b. hopeful
   c. unwilling
   d. impenetrable

9. *importune*
   a. curse
   b. beg
   c. impose
   d. suppose

10. *inadvertence*
    a. inaccuracy
    b. intentional
    c. willful
    d. oversight

(1-d; 2-d; 3-b; 4-d; 5-b; 6-d; 7-b; 8-d; 9-b; 10-d)

Drill 26

Choose the word that best completes the meaning of the sentence.

1. Since its _____, the company has put a premium on customer service.
   a. induction
   b. indictment
   c. ineptitude
   d. inception

2. Qualities such as trustworthiness, _____ as they may be, cannot be underestimated.
   a. intangible
   b. intrepid
   c. intransigent
   d. innocuous

3. The pain was so _____ that the most powerful drugs couldn't alleviate it.
   a. insatiable
   b. intractable
   c. introvert
   d. inscrutable

4. The ambassador's remarks were _____; they are sure to increase hostilities, not dispel them.
   a. inverse
   b. invidious
   c. integral
   d. ironic

5. The student tried to _____ himself by constantly commenting on the professor's wisdom.
   a. inhibit
   b. interpolate
   c. ingratiate
   d. inveigh

(1-d; 2-a; 3-b; 4-b; 5-c)

Drill 27

Match each word on the right with its definition in the left-hand column.

1. a coming to	a. abduction
2. a flowing together	b. fortitude
3. something added to	c. consequence
4. coming back to life	d. confluence
5. truthfulness	e. status
6. result	f. disunity
7. strength	g. veracity
8. lack of oneness	h. revival
9. a leading away	i. advent
10. standing	j. adjunct

(1-i; 2-d; 3-j; 4-h; 5-g; 6-c; 7-b; 8-f; 9-a; 10-e)

Drill 28

Choose the word that best completes the meaning of the sentence.

1. Her answers were quick and _____. She certainly knew her subject thoroughly.
   a. fallible
   b. facile
   c. fatuous
   d. feasible

2. His long-winded anecdotes were annoying; they were not always _____ to the topic.
   a. gratuitous
   b. generic
   c. genial
   d. germane

3. Those were the _____ days of childhood, carefree and playful.
   a. heinous
   b. hindsight
   c. harassing
   d. halcyon

4. The new employee was definitely _____. His ideas directly opposed those of the owner.
   a. inalienable
   b. iconoclastic
   c. ignoble
   d. illegible

5. It is _____ that you see the doctor if the symptoms persist.
   a. incessant
   b. illicit
   c. imperative
   d. impeccable

(1-b; 2-d; 3-d; 4-b; 5-c)

J

jeer	to mock, taunt
jejune	immature; insubstantial
jeopardy	risk, danger
jettison	to throw overboard
jocose	humorous, playful, full of goodwill
judicious	wise and careful, prudent, showing sound judgment
juxtaposition	to put side by side or close together

K

kindred	relatives, kin
kinetic	pertaining to motion or movement
knead	to massage

L

labyrinth	maze; confusing, complex arrangement or layout
lacerate	to tear, rip; to mangle
laconic	terse in speech or expression
languid	listless; indifferent
languish	to become weak; to lose health
lassitude	listlessness; weariness
latent	present but invisible or inactive, lying hidden and undeveloped
laudable	praiseworthy
lax	not strict, without firm discipline or limitations

legacy	bequest, something transmitted by a predecessor or ancestor
legitimate	lawful, sanctioned
lethargic	drowsy; slow-moving
levity	humor; frivolity
liable	legally obligated; responsible
liaison	link or connection between parts of a whole
libel	defamation in print or electronic broadcast
litigation	lawsuit
longevity	long lifespan
longitudinal	pertaining to length
loquacious	very talkative, chatty
lucid	transparent; clear; easily understood
lucrative	highly profitable
ludicrous	absurd; deserving to be laughed at
lugubrious	mournful, morose, sad
lurid	shocking, tastelessly sensational

Drill 29

Choose the word that best completes the meaning of the sentence.

1. _____ courage comes to the fore quickly in a crisis.
   a. Liable   c. Languid
   b. Latent   d. Lax

2. Don't put yourself in financial _____ by taking out another loan.
   a. jeopardy   c. juxtaposition
   b. jocoseness   d. judiciousness

3. My companion's tales were _____ and terribly depressing.
   a. lucrative   c. lucid
   b. lugubrious   d. lurid

4. A _____ passenger on a long flight soon becomes annoying.
   a. lethargic   c. laconic
   b. laudable   d. loquacious

5. I will serve as the _____ between the two groups.
   a. kindred   c. liaison
   b. labyrinth   d. lassitude

(1-b; 2-a; 3-b; 4-d; 5-c)

Drill 30

Match each word on the right with its definition in the left-hand column.

1. sum paid yearly	a. infinity
2. throwing out	b. duplicity
3. shortness	c. levity
4. endlessness	d. brevity
5. killing of a race	e. ejection
6. lightness of spirit	f. edict
7. a breaking	g. infraction
8. double-dealing	h. genocide
9. official decree	i. annuity
10. miniature world	j. microcosm

(1-i; 2-e; 3-d; 4-a; 5-h; 6-c; 7-g; 8-b; 9-f; 10-j)

M

macabre	gruesome; ghastly
magisterial	authoritative; official
magnanimous	noble-minded; benevolent
magnitude	pertaining to size
malfeasance	misconduct; wrongdoing, especially by an official
malign	to speak critically and cruelly of someone
malleable	easy to mold into various shapes, pliant
mandate	authoritative written command
manifest	to reveal, make evident
mar	to injure or damage by scratching or scraping
materiel	tools and equipment needed for a job or project
median	the middle or intermediate point
mediocre	ordinary, average; undistinguished
mellifluent	sounding sweet and smooth
mendacious	false, dishonest
meretricious	attractive in a flashy way; tawdry
meritorious	deserving reward or commendation
militate	to work against, present opposition
minuscule	very small, tiny, minute
misanthropy	cynical distrust of people
mitigate	to make milder, less severe, or less painful
mnemonics	system of memory improvement by using certain techniques
modulate	to tone down, adjust
mollify	to soothe, pacify, appease

morale	mental dynamic within a group regarding discipline, confidence, enthusiasm, and cooperation
morass	marsh or swamp; difficult situation
mordant	biting, sarcastic
moribund	dying
morose	gloomy; sullen; depressing
mundane	worldly; everyday, common
mutation	change
myopia	nearsightedness

N

nadir	the lowest point
nebulous	cloudy; vague
negate	to cancel, contradict; to make ineffective
negligible	insignificant, unimportant, trifling
neophyte	new convert; beginner
neutralize	to take away power, force, or strength
nihilism	belief that there is no meaning or purpose in existence
noctambulism	sleepwalking
nonchalant	casually indifferent; unconcerned
nonpareil	without equal or peer
non sequitur	remark having no bearing on what has just been said
novice	beginner; someone new to an occupation or activity
noxious	harmful, injurious
nullify	to cancel, make void

Drill 31

Choose the word or phrase that means most nearly the same as the *italicized* word.

1. *nadir*
   a. nonchalance
   b. survivor
   c. low point
   d. apex

2. *median*
   a. middle
   b. maximum
   c. foreign
   d. poorly constructed

3. *meretricious*
   a. praiseworthy
   b. dishonest
   c. superficially attractive
   d. impecunious

4. *militate*
   a. work against
   b. arm
   c. attack
   d. debate

5. *kinetic*
   a. paralyzed
   b. cow-like
   c. motion
   d. frightening

6. *mnemonics*
   a. memory development
   b. forgetfulness
   c. ammunition
   d. painkillers

7. *morass*
   a. field
   b. mountain range
   c. inundation
   d. swamp

8. *mellifluent*
   a. bilingual
   b. sweet
   c. aphasic
   d. ill-willed

9. *mutation*
   a. silence
   b. purification
   c. flux
   d. change

10. *negate*
    a. mock
    b. make ineffective
    c. transmute
    d. weigh down

(1-c; 2-a; 3-c; 4-a; 5-c; 6-a; 7-d; 8-b; 9-d; 10-b)

Drill 32

Choose the word that best completes the meaning of the sentence.

1. A young child's mind is _____. Be careful of the example you set!
   a. modulated   c. malleable
   b. macabre   d. magisterial

2. Such distrust and cynicism are _____.
   a. misanthropic   c. mar
   b. magnanimous   d. meritorious

3. His worries made him a _____ and lugubrious companion.
   a. morose   c. mediocre
   b. morass   d. minuscule

4. Associating someone's name with a physical trait is a _____ device many find beneficial.
   a. meretricious   c. mendacious
   b. mnemonic   d. mellifluent

5. I will not be _____ by such attempts to make good on your mistakes!
   a. mollified   c. militated
   b. mitigated   d. mutated

(1-c; 2-a; 3-a; 4-b; 5-a)

Drill 33

Choose the word or phrase that means most nearly the same as the *italicized* word.

1. *harass*
   a. annoy
   b. tether
   c. litigate
   d. propose

2. *lacerate*
   a. cover with oil
   b. chew
   c. tear roughly
   d. fling

3. *legacy*
   a. summons
   b. inheritance
   c. written document
   d. affidavit

4. *liable*
   a. deceptive
   b. owned by
   c. prone
   d. obligated

5. *litigation*
   a. fury
   b. lawsuit
   c. constraint
   d. happenstance

6. *lucid*
   a. ridiculous
   b. lightweight
   c. transparent
   d. not bound

7. *lugubrious*
   a. mournful
   b. laughable
   c. deeply cut
   d. accented

8. *idiosyncrasy*
   a. nervousness
   b. clownishness
   c. defect
   d. peculiarity

9. *malfeasance*
   a. wrongdoing
   b. maliciousness
   c. disowning
   d. sorrowfulness

10. *manifest*
    a. make clear
    b. holiday
    c. varied
    d. make straight

(1-a; 2-c; 3-b; 4-d; 5-b; 6-c; 7-a; 8-d; 9-a; 10-a)

4

English
A Rich and Varied Language

As language is the palpable form of thinking, it is important that you understand, in our global community, how languages interact and differ. English may be the official international language of almost all communication, but a deeper understanding of how your language works will give you insight into how it is understood.

Modern American English is a complex, dynamic, and extremely colorful language. Unlike most languages, English is actually the end result of the forced merging of Latinate and Germanic vocabularies, and so it has almost double the number of words actually needed for basic speech. We have innumerable examples of double or even triple words for almost the same idea: "forecast," "prediction," "prognostication." As we move up to socially and academically "higher" level words, we move from the basic Germanic word to the Latinate to the Greek.

English is also an extremely "elastic" language, capable of absorbing new words from all sources and making them

"English." "Shampoo" is Hindi; "raccoon" is AmerIndian; "poltergeist" is German; "boondock" is from the Philippines; "landscape" is Dutch; "algebra" is Arabic — a great proportion of our "English" words are from times and places far away from the 21st century.

And English frequently takes names and concepts from history, religion, and literature, to create new words that capture for all time the essence of that person or event — "quisling" now means traitor; "armageddon" conjures up images of final destruction.

One of the most creative aspects of the English language is its willingness to absorb unchanged foreign words pertaining to particular fields of endeavor. There are no precise words in pure "English" that can better describe fashion or cuisine than the French terms we have borrowed, or than the Italian words used in musical composition. Also, English has kept many Latin words and phrases intact. This chapter should open your eyes to the richness of English in "borrowed" words from so many other languages.

FOREIGN TERMS

a cappella	It. without accompaniment
à la carte	F. priced separately
adagio	It. slow
ad hoc	L. for a specific, limited purpose
ad nauseam	L. to a ridiculous or disgusting degree
agitato	It. agitated
al fresco	It. outdoors
allegro	It. lively, fast
alto	It. low female voice
andante	It. moving steadily
aria	It. operatic song
arpeggio	It. broken chord
avant-garde	F. at the forefront of a field; ahead of the times
basso	It. low male voice
bête noire	F. "black beast"; something you especially dislike or avoid
blasé	F. bored from overindulgence
bonbon	F. small candy
bonhomie	F. good-natured
bon mot	F. clever saying
bon vivant	F. one who enjoys the "good life" of luxury
bouquet garni	F. mixture of finely chopped herbs tied in a small cotton bag and added to cooking food

bourgeois   F. middle-class

bravura   It. technically difficult

cantabile   It. flowing and lyrical

cantata   It. work for chorus and orchestra

cantina   Sp. saloon

capriccio   It. spirited

cause célèbre   F. popular cause or issue

caveat emptor   L. "Let the buyer beware."

chef d'œuvre   F. masterpiece

coda   It. concluding section

coiffure   F. hairstyle

con brio   It. with spirit

concerto   It. work for solo instrument and orchestra

cordon bleu   F. blue ribbon

coup de grâce   F. "stroke of mercy"; the final blow

crescendo   It. becoming louder

cul-de-sac   F. dead end

de facto   L. actual, in reality

déjà vu   F. already seen; feeling that one is reliving a past experience

denouement   F. unraveling or solution of a play or book's plot

détente   F. relaxing or easing of relations

deus ex machina   L. contrived, improbable agent which solves a situation

Dies Irae   L. Judgment Day

diminuendo	It. becoming quieter
divertissement	F. diversion, amusement
dolce	It. sweetly
double-entendre	F. term with two meanings
éclat	F. brilliant achievement
élan	F. flair, style
en croûte	F. baked in pastry crust
en passant	F. in passing; by the way
entrepreneur	F. business owner
ex officio	L. by virtue of office or position
fait accompli	F. accomplished fact
falsetto	It. very high male voice
faux pas	F. "false step"; a socially embarrassing mistake
finale	It. final movement
fin de siècle	F. turn-of-the-century
fiambé	F. food coated with liquor and ignited before serving
florentine	F. served with spinach
forte	It. loud
fortissimo	It. very loud
gauche	F. "left-handed"; clumsy, inept
impasse	F. dead end, dilemma
ingenue	F. innocent, naive young woman

insouciance	F. carefree indifference
intermezzo	It. short interlude
ipso facto	L. by the very fact
julienne	F. cut in long, thin strips
junta	Sp. council; group of political intriguers
laissez-faire	F. noninterference
largo	It. slow
legato	It. smooth
lento	It. slow
magnum opus	L. masterpiece
malaise	F. vague feeling of illness or depression
mélange	F. mixture
missa	It. Mass
mot juste	F. the appropriate thing to say
noblesse oblige	F. honorable behavior expected of someone of high birth or rank
nom de plume	F. pen name, pseudonym
non sequitur	L. illogical statement that doesn't "follow" what was just said
nouveau riche	F. one who suddenly and ostentatiously has wealth
par excellence	F. epitome of something
parvenu	F. sudden newcomer to the upper class

pâtisserie	F. bakery
pianissimo	It. very soft
piano	It. soft
pièce de résistance	F. outstanding accomplishment
piquant	F. spicy, pungent
poco	It. a little
potpourri	F. stew; miscellany
presto	It. fast, quickly
pro forma	L. as a matter of form or custom
quid pro quo	L. exact exchange or substitution
quod erat demonstratum (Q.E.D.)	L. which was to be demonstrated or proved
rapprochement	F. formal reconciliation
repartee	F. swift, witty reply
répondez s'il vous plaît (R.S.V.P.)	F. please reply
sangfroid	F. "cold blood"; dispassionate, cool-headed
sauté	F. to cook quickly in a small amount of butter and oil over a high flame
savoir faire	F. tact, skill at always doing the proper thing

sempre	It. always
sine die	L. indefinitely
sine qua non	L. essential part or condition
sonata	It. composition for piano and/or solo instrument
soprano	It. high female voice
soupçon	F. trace; suspicion
staccato	It. abrupt, short notes
tempo	It. speed
tête-à-tête	F. "head-to-head"; intimate meeting
tour de force	F. feat of strength or brilliance
tutti	It. all
vaquero	Sp. cowboy
Véronique	F. garnish of cooked seedless green grapes
vignette	F. sketch or scene
virtuoso	It. one who excels in the practice of an art
vivace	It. lively
voce	It. voice

Drill 34

Match the foreign term in the right-hand column with its meaning on the left.

<table>
<tr><td>1. noninterference</td><td>a. adagio</td></tr>
<tr><td>2. trace, suspicion</td><td>b. fait accompli</td></tr>
<tr><td>3. spicy, pungent</td><td>c. al fresco</td></tr>
<tr><td>4. something disliked, avoided</td><td>d. bon mot</td></tr>
<tr><td></td><td>e. sine qua non</td></tr>
<tr><td>5. an accomplished fact</td><td>f. soupçon</td></tr>
<tr><td>6. outdoors</td><td>g. laissez-faire</td></tr>
<tr><td>7. essential part or condition</td><td>h. piquant</td></tr>
<tr><td>8. slow</td><td>i. en passant</td></tr>
<tr><td>9. clever saying</td><td>j. bête noire</td></tr>
<tr><td>10. by the way</td><td></td></tr>
</table>

(1-g; 2-f; 3-h; 4-j; 5-b; 6-c; 7-e; 8-a; 9-d; 10-i)

Drill 35

Match the foreign term in the right-hand column with its meaning on the left.

1. easing relations	a. legato
2. vague illness or depression	b. forte
	c. bourgeois
3. actual, in reality	d. éclat
4. swift, witty reply	e. malaise
5. bakery	f. de facto
6. loud	g. détente
7. middle-class	h. repartee
8. coolheadedness	i. pâtisserie
9. brilliant achievement	j. sangfroid
10. smooth	

(1-g; 2-e; 3-f; 4-h; 5-i; 6-b; 7-c; 8-j; 9-d; 10-a)

Drill 36

Match each foreign term in the right-hand column with its meaning on the left.

1. exact exchange or substitution	a. parvenu
	b. impasse
2. reconciliation	c. divertissement
3. dilemma	d. quid pro quo
4. clumsy	e. faux pas
5. served with spinach	f. staccato
6. an amusement	g. gauche
7. social newcomer	h. vignette
8. social mistake	i. rapprochement
9. abrupt, sharp notes	j. florentine
10. sketch or scene	

(1-d; 2-i; 3-b; 4-g; 5-j; 6-c; 7-a; 8-e; 9-f; 10-h)

ABBREVIATIONS

It's not just words alone that you'll encounter in your reading and writing. Here's a list of common abbreviations and special terms you will want to know, many of them borrowed from Latin.

A.D.	(*anno Domini*) after Christ
a.k.a.	also known as
a.m.	(*ante meridiem*) before noon
A.W.O.L.	absent without official leave
B.C.	before Christ
bldg.	building
blvd.	boulevard
ca (c.)	(*circa*) about
cf.	(*confer*) compare
C.O.D.	cash on delivery
cv	curriculum vitae
db	decibel
d.b.a.	doing business as
e.g.	(*exempli gratia*) for example
et al.	(*et alii*) and others
etc.	(*et cetera*) and so forth
f., ff.	and the following page(s)
hp.	horsepower
ibid.	(*ibidem*) in the same place
i.e.	(*id est*) that is (to say)
loc. cit.	(*loco citato*) in the place cited
M	(*mil*) one thousand

ms., mss.	manuscript(s)
n.b.	(*nota bene*) mark well
op. cit.	(*opere citato*) in the work cited
p.m.	(*post meridiem*) after noon
p., pp.	page(s)
pro tem	(*pro tempore*) temporarily
p.s.i.	pounds per square inch
q.v.	(*quod vide*) which see
r.p.m.	revolutions per minute
s/h	shipping and handling
t.	ton
v	volt
v.i.	(*vide infra*) see below
viz	(*videlicet*) namely
vs.	(*versus*) as against, in contrast to
v.s.	(*vide supra*) see above

WORDS FROM LITERATURE, MYTHOLOGY, AND HISTORY

adonis   vain and beautiful man — from Adonis, youth loved by Aphrodite in Greek mythology

bacchanal   wild, uninhibited orgy — from Bacchus, Greek god of wine

bloomers   loose, gathered pants for women — named after 19th century American feminist Amelia Bloomer

bowdlerize   to edit prudishly — named after Thomas Bowdler, 18th century Englishman who tried to expurgate the works of Shakespeare

boycott   to abstain in protest as a form of coercion — named after a 19th century Irish land agent who had refused to lower rents

cassandra   prophet doomed to be ignored — from Cassandra, Trojan princess and prophetess who was never believed

chauvinism   militant and fanatical loyalty — named after Nicholas Chauvin, a devoted follower of Napoleon

draconian   severe, harsh measures — named after Draco, a particularly harsh Athenian lawgiver

erotic   pertaining to sexual love — from Eros, Greek god of sexual love

galvanize   to stimulate with electricity; to startle into action — named after Luigi Galvani, Italian scientist

halcyon   peaceful, prosperous times — named after the mythical bird that nested at sea at the time of the winter solstice and calmed the waves

herculean   requiring tremendous effort — from Hercules, mythical Greek hero renowned for his strength

hermetic   secret; sealed — from Hermes, the Greek messenger god

hydra   complicated problem that must be solved from many different perspectives — from Hydra, a many-headed monster in Greek mythology

junoesque   stately, imposing beauty — from Juno, Roman goddess of women and queen of heaven

lilliputian   of small intelligence, tiny — named after the tiny people in Jonathan Swift's *Gulliver's Travels*

lothario   seducer — named after a character in the play *The Fair Penitent* by Nicholas Rowe

lynch   to execute or hang without trial — named after Charles Lynch, 18th century justice of the peace in Virginia

machiavellian   politically expedient, regardless of people's needs or rights — named after Niccolo Machiavelli, author of *The Prince*

martinet   rigid, militaristic disciplinarian — named after Jean Martinet, 19th century French general

maverick   nonconformist — named after Samuel Maverick, 19th century Texas rancher who refused to brand his cattle

mercurial   changeable; swift — from Mercury, Roman god of travel and cunning

mesmerize   to hypnotize — named after Franz Mesmer, 18th century Austrian doctor who developed the technique

narcissistic self-absorbed; exceedingly vain — from Nar-
cissus, youth in Greek mythology who falls
in love with his own reflection

nemesis deadly adversary — from Nemesis, Greek
goddess of retributive justice

odyssey long, wandering adventure; a search — named
after *The Odyssey,* Homer's epic poem about
the wanderings of King Odysseus

olympian something very majestic — named after Mt.
Olympus in Greece

pander to pimp; to appeal to someone's lowest
instincts — named after Pandarus, the go-
between in Geoffrey Chaucer's *Troilus and
Criseyde*

philippic virulent condemnation — named after a series
of speeches given by the Greek philosopher
Demosthenes against Philip of Macedon

phoenix something reborn from its own destruction —
from the legendary bird that burned itself on
a pyre and rose alive from the ashes

promethean boldly creative; inspirational; life-giving —
from Prometheus, a figure in Greek mythol-
ogy who steals fire from heaven and gives it
to humankind

protean variable; versatile; creative — from Proteus,
the Greek sea god, who was capable of tak-
ing on different forms

pyrrhic victory won with staggering losses — named
after Pyrrhus, who sustained many losses
after a bloody battle between the Epireans
and Romans

quixotic	blindly idealistic and romantic — named after Miguel Cervantes's famous *Don Quixote de la Mancha*
sadism	delight in cruelty — named after the perverse French nobleman, the Marquis de Sade
saturnine	gloomy, taciturn — from the Roman god Saturn
stentorian	loud, deep voice — named after Stentor, herald in the Trojan War
tantalize	to torment with unattainable things — from Tantalus, legendary king of Lydia who was punished by being made to stand in a pool beneath a bough of fruit, unable to either drink or eat
titanic	powerful; huge — named after the Titans, who were mythical giants
vandal	someone who willfully destroys property — named after the Vandals, a Germanic tribe that ravaged Europe during the Dark Ages

Drill 37

Match each word in the left-hand column with one on the right.

1.	tantalize	a.	majestic
2.	titanic	b.	powerful
3.	hermetic	c.	prophet doomed to be
4.	odyssey		ignored
5.	promethean	d.	exceedingly vain
6.	olympian	e.	creative
7.	saturnine	f.	to torment
8.	nemesis	g.	deadly adversary
9.	cassandra	h.	secret, sealed
10.	narcissistic	i.	a search
		j.	gloomy

(1-f; 2-b; 3-h; 4-i; 5-e; 6-a; 7-j; 8-g; 9-c; 10-d)

ESSENTIAL VOCABULARY IV

O

obdurate	hardened; stubbornly resistant
obeisance	reverential behavior or gestures
obfuscate	to muddle intentionally, confuse
objective	(*adj.*) impersonal; unbiased (*n.*) aim, goal
obliterate	to erase, blot out; to destroy
oblivious	unaware of, not noticing something
obloquy	public disgrace; infamy
obscure	dim; unclear; murky
obsequious	overly submissive; fawning
obsess	to be haunted by or fixated on something
obsolete	outmoded; no longer in use or practice
obstreperous	boisterous, unruly; argumentative
obtrude	to impose or force something unwanted upon others
obtuse	blunted; dull
obviate	to do away with, prevent; make unnecessary
occidental	native of the western world (occident), not oriental
oleaginous	oily; slippery
omnipotent	all-powerful
onerous	burdensome; full of heavy responsibility
onus	responsibility for a wrong
opprobrium	reproach; contempt
optimum	the best or most favorable
orbicular	pertaining to a sphere or circle

ordinance   city statute

orifice   mouth; opening, aperture

oscillate   to swing or move back and forth in a regular pattern

ostensible   apparent, seemingly obvious

ostentatious   pretentious, showy

Drill 38

Choose the word that best completes the meaning of the sentence.

1. The odor was so _____ that the customers rushed to leave the store.
   a. neurotic
   b. nebulous
   c. noxious
   d. nocturnal

2. That model is _____. We discontinued it four years ago.
   a. obsolete
   b. onerous
   c. obtuse
   d. obdurate

3. When the engine was turned on, the pendulum began to _____.
   a. obviate
   b. oscillate
   c. obliterate
   d. obfuscate

4. The _____ reason for doing it is that it's obviously the best solution.
   a. ostentatious
   b. optional
   c. oblivious
   d. ostensible

5. The convicted felon was _____ even after receiving such a harsh sentence.
   a. obdurate
   b. obtuse
   c. onerous
   d. omnipotent

(1-c; 2-a; 3-b; 4-d; 5-a)

Drill 39

Match each foreign term in the right-hand column with its meaning on the left.

1. naive young woman	a. crescendo
2. mixture	b. mot juste
3. becoming louder	c. savoir faire
4. for a specific, limited purpose	d. ingenue
	e. denouement
5. appropriate thing to say	f. insouciance
6. flair	g. ad hoc
7. final movement	h. mélange
8. tact	i. élan
9. solution of plot	j. finale
10. carefree indifference	

(1-d; 2-h; 3-a; 4-g; 5-b; 6-i; 7-j; 8-c; 9-e; 10-f)

P

pacific	peaceful, tranquil, calm
palliate	to lessen, alleviate, ease
palpitate	to beat rapidly or flutter
panacea	supposed cure for all diseases
paradigm	pattern or model to be copied, template
paradox	statement that contains contradictory ideas or concepts
paraphrase	brief rewording; synopsis
parity	state of being equal
paroxysm	spasm of pain
parsimony	miserliness, stinginess
partisan	devoted to a cause
peccadillo	minor sin; slight fault
pecuniary	pertaining to money
pedantic	pompous display of learning, but little wisdom
penchant	inclination; tendency
penurious	stingy
perambulate	to walk around, amble
perceive	to notice, comprehend
peremptory	something unchangeable, not to be delayed or denied
peripheral	along the edge; incidental, not central
permeable	able to be penetrated or passed through, especially by fluids
pernicious	destructive, noxious, threatening
perpendicular	at right angles to something else

perpetrate	to do, perform, commit; to be guilty of
personnel	employees
perspicuous	lucid; easily understood
peruse	to read or study carefully or thoroughly
pervious	able to be penetrated or permeated
petulant	sulky, irritable; impatient
placate	to appease, calm down
placid	tranquil, calm
plenary	fully attended
pontificate	to speak in a pompous or dogmatic way
portentous	foretelling; ominous; amazing
posterity	future generations
precarious	risky; not secure
precedent	example, reason, or justification for something that follows
precipitous	steep, cliff-like
preclude	to make impossible or unnecessary
precocious	developed or advanced beyond one's age
precursor	forerunner; harbinger
predicament	difficult, embarrassing, or problematic situation
predilection	partiality or preference; inclination
prejudice	biased or uninformed opinion
prerogative	special right or privilege
presume	to claim or assume without permission or authority
prevaricate	to evade the truth
primordial	existing at or from the beginning

principal	first in rank, authority, importance, or degree
principle	fundamental truth, law, or doctrine
probity	honesty; uprightness, integrity
proclivity	tendency, inclination
procure	to get, obtain
prodigious	of great size, power, or effort
profligate	shameless; dissolute
prolix	long-winded; wordy
propinquity	nearness in time or place
proscribe	to outlaw
prototype	first model, archetype
protract	to draw out, prolong
protuberance	bulge, swelling
proximity	nearness in time or place
punctilious	meticulous; careful about every detail
pusillanimous	timid, fainthearted; cowardly
putative	reputed, assumed or accepted to be as such

Drill 40

Choose the word or phrase most nearly **opposite** in meaning to the *italicized* word.

1. *impunity*
   a. sullied
   b. ignorance
   c. punishment
   d. without hope

2. *laconic*
   a. watery
   b. musical
   c. vivacious
   d. verbose

3. *languid*
   a. fluent
   b. moist
   c. sickly
   d. vigorous

4. *lassitude*
   a. tangle
   b. long-windedness
   c. determination
   d. vitality

5. *profligate*
   a. poor
   b. illegal
   c. shameless
   d. forgetful

6. *obfuscate*
   a. lame
   b. placate
   c. adulterate
   d. clarify

7. *instigate*
   a. begin
   b. placate
   c. discover
   d. imply

8. *petulant*
   a. irascible
   b. cheerful
   c. uncouth
   d. abnormal

9. *lurid*
   a. placid
   b. clear
   c. deceived
   d. transparent

10. *obsequious*
    a. respectful
    b. bold
    c. hereditary
    d. murky

(1-c; 2-d; 3-d; 4-d; 5-a; 6-d; 7-b; 8-b; 9-a; 10-b)

Drill 41

Choose the word or phrase most nearly **opposite** in meaning to the *italicized* word.

1. myopic
   a. nervous
   b. far-sighted
   c. telepathic
   d. rotted

2. lucrative
   a. debasing
   b. unprofitable
   c. influential
   d. monetary

3. ostensible
   a. showy
   b. unapparent
   c. rust-free
   d. blended

4. emollient
   a. calming
   b. insulting
   c. abrasive
   d. toxic

5. oleaginous
   a. sweet
   b. dry
   c. soothing
   d. disgruntled

(1-b; 2-b; 3-b; 4-d; 5-b)

Drill 42

Choose the word that best completes the meaning of the sentence.

1. She was a _____ of the successful and shrewd manager.
   - a. paradox
   - b. paradigm
   - c. paraphrase
   - d. paroxysm

2. The old man had a _____ for cigars, even though his doctor had forbidden them.
   - a. peccadillo
   - b. panacea
   - c. parity
   - d. penchant

3. Around the _____ of the park, they planted dozens of fir trees.
   - a. periphery
   - b. posterity
   - c. perpendicular
   - d. peremptory

4. The child was certainly _____ to be playing the violins so well at three years old.
   - a. precursor
   - b. precocious
   - c. prejudiced
   - d. precipitous

5. I need clear answers to my questions — do not _____!
   - a. preclude
   - b. precede
   - c. prevaricate
   - d. procure

(1-b; 2-d; 3-a; 4-b; 5-c)

Q

quagmire	swamp; difficult position
quandary	doubt, uncertainty, dilemma
query	to ask questions
quiescent	calmed; undisturbed
quintessence	pure essence or perfect example of something
quota	proportional share
quotidian	daily

R

rampant	widespread, rife, epidemic
rancor	long-standing and bitter hatred or ill will
ratify	formal agreement or vote
ratio	fixed relation in degree or number
rationale	fundamental reasons or argument for something
raze	to knock down and destroy
rebuke	to reprimand or scold sharply
rebuttal	contradiction; reply to a charge or argument
recalcitrant	stubborn; obstructionist; refusing to obey
recapitulate	to repeat briefly; to summarize
reconcile	to bring back together, make friendly again
recourse	that to which one turns when seeking aid or safety
recriminate	to answer an accusation with another one
rectitude	integrity, uprightness, strict honesty
recur	to return

redeem	to get back; to justify
redress	to make compensation or satisfaction for something wrong
refrain	to hold back, abstain from
regimen	daily routine or schedule
reiterate	to repeat again and again
relegate	to consign or assign to a lower position
remit	to pardon; to send in payment
renege	to go back on a promise or an agreement
renounce	to give up or repudiate
reprehend	to disapprove of, criticize
repress	to hold back, restrain, subdue
reprimand	formal rebuke by someone in authority
reprove	to censure
repudiate	to denounce, refuse to be associated with
rescind	to revoke, repeal, cancel
resilient	capable of springing back
restitution	giving back something lost or taken away, restoration
reticent	restrained, quiet, understated; reluctant to speak
retroactive	going into effect as of a specified date in the past
rife	widespread, prevalent
risibility	sense of the ridiculous or amusing
ruminate	to ponder; to chew

Drill 43

Choose the word or phrase that means most nearly the same as the *italicized* word.

1. *paroxysm*
   a. pain
   b. laughter
   c. numbness
   d. revolt

2. *rebuttal*
   a. knock again
   b. refusal
   c. contradiction
   d. controversy

3. *recapitulate*
   a. invade
   b. procure
   c. summarize
   d. truncate

4. *reconcile*
   a. bring to agreement
   b. reconsider
   c. ponder
   d. bring to fruition

5. *recriminate*
   a. incarcerate
   b. reprobate
   c. counteraccuse
   d. countermand

6. *prolix*
   a. wordy
   b. nearby
   c. pointed
   d. tasty

7. *relegate*
   a. enact as law
   b. reread
   c. assign to lower position
   d. turn over

8. *reprehend*
   a. blame
   b. remember
   c. grasp
   d. eject

9. *raze*
   a. lift up
   b. burnish
   c. knock down
   d. skim off

10. *rescind*
    a. cancel
    b. burn
    c. raise
    d. return

(1-a; 2-c; 3-c; 4-a; 5-c; 6-a; 7-c; 8-a; 9-c; 10-a)

Drill 44

Choose the word that best completes the meaning of the sentence.

1. We were in a _____ when we were invited to three parties on the same evening!
   a. quagmire
   b. quandary
   c. query
   d. quintessence

2. His _____, after so many years, could not be softened.
   a. rancor
   b. recourse
   c. rebuttal
   d. rebuke

3. I cannot trust people once I find out they've _____ on a promise.
   a. remitted
   b. redressed
   c. refrained
   d. reneged

4. The student was _____ and uneasy during oral examinations.
   a. reticent
   b. rife
   c. relegated
   d. repudiated

5. The virus was _____ in the tropical regions, infecting all who ventured beyond the city.
   a. rescind
   b. retroactive
   c. rife
   d. reticent

(1-b; 2-a; 3-d; 4-a; 5-c)

Drill 45

Choose the word or phrase that means most nearly the same as the *italicized* word.

1. modulate
   a. upgrade
   b. alter
   c. tone down
   d. improve

2. nonchalant
   a. unattainable
   b. excitable
   c. nonessential
   d. indifferent

3. nonpareil
   a. insane
   b. crooked
   c. without equal
   d. delated

4. magnanimous
   a. insolent
   b. shrewd
   c. unselfish
   d. threatening

5. morose
   a. curious
   b. gloomy
   c. impatient
   d. timid

(1-c; 2-d; 3-c; 4-c; 5-b)

Drill 46

Match each word in the left-hand column with its definition on the right.

1. galvanize	a. harsh condemnation
2. maverick	b. to edit prudishly
3. martinet	c. fanatical loyalty
4. quixotic	d. politically expedient
5. chauvinism	e. nonconformist
6. bowdlerize	f. severe, harsh measures
7. machiavellian	g. rigid disciplinarian
8. philippic	h. to startle into action
9. pyrrhic	i. won at a great price
10. draconian	j. idealistic and romantic

(1-h; 2-e; 3-g; 4-j; 5-c; 6-b; 7-d; 8-a; 9-i; 10-f)

5

English
Today's Global Language

In Chapter 4 you learned how everyday English has been shaped by other languages around the world and from the past. Now, you will see how English has become the dominant global language for communicating essential economic, technological, and political developments.

Because of its precision, flexibility, and sheer size, English is a "gateway" language for language speakers worldwide. It is the most sought-after second language in the world—close to half a billion people speak English as their first or second language. In Japan alone, according to a *Wall Street Journal* estimate, nearly ten million people either are looking for or are enrolled in English conversation classes. It is the acknowledged international language of transportation, finance, business, computer programming, and mass communications, and the de facto language of almost every other form of human activity. It has even supplanted French as the language of diplomacy.

French may still be the language of fashion and cuisine, and Italian of the arts, but English is the language used worldwide to communicate in almost every area of human activity. As information transfer becomes global and instantaneous, the English language is increasingly being used as the prime vehicle. Those who have command of English will have greater access to global information.

You will begin to see the cutting-edge qualities of English in this chapter. Not only are these specialized vocabularies extremely precise and specific to a particular field of knowledge, but also they embody the dynamic nature of English. As new concepts are presented and technological developments occur, English is quick to coin a new word or phrase that will be accepted internationally. What you read as news one day will be absorbed into our vocabulary the next. This is the English that captures the future.

THE WORD COMPONENTS OF MEDICINE

Suffixes

-agra	seizure of pain
-ectomy	removal of
-emia	blood condition
-genic	produced or caused by
-graph	recording or tracing device
-ia	condition
-iasis	diseased
-in (-ine)	chemical substance
-itis (-itic)	inflammation
-lysis	breaking down
-oma	swelling, tumor
-opia	eye, sight
-osis (-otic)	diseased
-pathy	disease or treatment of
-rrhea (-rrhage)	discharge
-therapy	treatment

Other Word Components

Characteristics

brachy	short
brady	slow
ecto	outer
endo	inner
hyper	high

hypo	low
scler	hard
tachy	fast

Colors

chlor	green
chrom	color
cyan	blue
erythr	red
leuk	white
melan	black
poli	gray
xanth	yellow

Parts of the Body

aden	gland
angi	vein
arthr	joint
bronch	windpipe
card	heart
cephal	head
chir	hand
chol	gall, bile
chondr	cartilage
crani	head, brain
cyst	bladder, sac
dactyl	finger, toe

derm	skin
enter	intestine
gastr	stomach
hemo/a	blood
hepat	liver
hyster	womb
larng	nose
mast	breast
my	muscle
mye	marrow
myel	spinal cord
neph	kidney
neuro/a	nerve
ophthalm	eye
oste	bone
phleb	blood vessel
pneu	lung, breath
ren	kidney
rhin	nose
stoma	mouth, opening
tox	poison
trache	windpipe
veno	vein
ventro	abdomen

Miscellaneous

alg	pain
burs	sac
cyt	cell
gangli	knot
glyc	sugar
hist	tissue
lip	fat
mening	membrane
noia	mind
pleg	paralysis
psor	itch
psych	mind
soma	body
tox	poison

Drill 47

Match each word on the left with its definition in the right-hand column.

1. psychotic
2. otorhino-laryngologist
3. hematoma
4. pericardium
5. hepatitis
6. gastroenteritis
7. leukemia
8. toxin
9. hemorrhage
10. brachydactylism

a. poisonous substance
b. abnormally short fingers
c. bruise
d. inflammation of the liver
e. abnormal discharge of blood
f. lining around the heart
g. diseased mind
h. ear, nose, and throat doctor
i. inflammation of stomach and intestines
j. diseased white blood cells

(1-g; 2-h; 3-c; 4-f; 5-d; 6-i; 7-j; 8-a; 9-e; 10-b)

Drill 48

Match each term in the right-hand column with its definition in the left-hand column.

1. inflammation of gray spinal matter
2. yellowish skin
3. low blood sugar
4. eye doctor
5. study of tissue cells

a. hypoglycemia
b. histology
c. poliomyelitis
d. ophthalmologist
e. xanthoderma

(1-c; 2-e; 3-a; 4-d; 5-b)

THE LANGUAGE OF LAW

abet	to incite to, sanction, or help in wrongdoing
abjure	to give up (rights, allegiance, etc.) on oath; to renounce
abscond	to flee suddenly to avoid prosecution or arrest
accessory	person who assists in a crime, while not participating in it
accomplice	one who knowingly participates in a crime
acquit	to release from duty or obligation
adjudication	legal judgment or ruling
adjure	to charge or command solemnly, often under oath or penalty
affidavit	sworn written statement signed before an authorized officer of the court such as a notary public
alibi	defensive excuse
altercation	heated argument or noisy quarrel
amicus curiae	(L. "friend of the court") one who, although not involved in a lawsuit, has enough interest in its outcome to be allowed to present an argument or introduce evidence by way of an amicus brief
appellate court	court that reviews cases and appeals pertaining to judgments reached by a trial court
arraignment	formal court appearance of a defendant, after an indictment has been filed, when charges, rights, and pleas are presented

arson	malicious setting afire of property
assault	attempt or threat to inflict bodily harm on another person
battery	unconsented use of physical force on another person
bequest	property given to someone in a will
breach	opening or gap; failure to keep the terms, as of a promise or law
citation	summons to appear in court; official praise, as for bravery; reference to legal precedent or authority
codicil	supplement or appendix to a will
collusion	secret agreement for fraudulent or illegal purposes; conspiracy
contiguous	sharing a boundary; adjacent
contraband	goods prohibited by law or treaty to be imported or exported
corpus delicti	(L. "the body of the crime") physical proof of a crime and criminal intent
defendant	person or party sued by the plaintiff in civil lawsuits
deposition	written record of a witness's sworn testimony before a trial
disenfranchise	to deprive of a right of citizenship, such as the right to vote

embezzlement	unauthorized use of funds of which one has lawful possession but not ownership
eminent domain	government's right to take private land for public use with payment of just compensation
equity	equitable right or claim; justice applied in circumstances not covered by law
ex post facto	(L. "after the fact") retroactive
extradition	legal surrender of an alleged criminal to another jurisdiction for trial
felony	serious crime punishable by imprisonment or death
fraud	intentional deceit or misrepresentation that cheats or harms another person
habeas corpus	(L. "you have the body") court-ordered writ demanding that a person being held in custody or imprisonment be brought before the court to determine the legality of the detainment
incarcerate	to put in jail
indictment	formal written criminal accusation needed by the grand jury to decide whether enough evidence exists to warrant a trial
injunction	court order enjoining or prohibiting someone from a specific action
inquest	judicial inquiry, as a coroner's investigation of a death

intestate   dying without leaving a will

jurisdiction   legal authority and/or geographical territory of a particular court

jurisprudence   science and philosophy of law

larceny   theft

libel   printed or broadcast statement.that is both false and damaging to someone's reputation

lien   financial claim on a piece of property belonging to someone

litigation   act or process of carrying on a lawsuit

manslaughter   unlawful killing of someone, but without premeditation or malice

misdemeanor   relatively minor criminal offense, usually punishable by a fine or short jail term

nolo contendere (L. "I do not wish to contend.") acceptance of the facts in an indictment, as opposed to a formal plea of guilty, on which the judge would pass judgment

non compos mentis   (L. "not of sound mind") legally insane or incompetent

nullify   to make legally null, void, annul

perjury   making a false statement under oath

perpetrator   one who commits a crime

plaintiff	person or group initiating a civil lawsuit
probate	procedure of determining the validity of a will and distributing the estate as indicated in the will
probation	nonprison sentence sometimes given after a defendant has been found guilty
pro bono publico	(L. "for the public good") free legal representation for a beneficial cause
pro se	(L. "for himself") representing oneself in court rather than retaining a lawyer
retainer	advance fee paid a lawyer for future services
statute	law enacted by federal or state legislation
subpoena	(L. "under penalty") court-ordered writ requiring a witness to attend a judicial proceeding
tort	noncontract violation of civil law that damages or injures another
tribunal	seat or court of justice
verdict	decision, esp. a legal judgment of guilt or innocence
warrant	written court order authorizing an act such as a search or an arrest

Drill 49

Choose the word that best completes each sentence.

1. The defendant stood before the judge during the _____ and listened to the charges.
   - a. arraignment
   - b. indictment
   - c. injunction
   - d. subpoena

2. By the time the police arrived at the bank to question the employee suspected of embezzlement, the teller had _____ with $5,000
   - a. fraud
   - b. absconded
   - c. assaulted
   - d. deposed

3. The reporter wanted the club owner charged with _____ for pushing her down the stairs.
   - a. altercation
   - b. battery
   - c. arson
   - d. manslaughter

4. When the police inspected the abandoned plane, they found that the smugglers had left behind most of the _____ during their hasty escape.
   - a. contraband
   - b. statute
   - c. equity
   - d. lien

5. The prosecutors were looking for the _____ who had knowlingly provided the car used in the hold-up.
   - a. defendent
   - b. accomplice
   - c. accessory
   - d. retainer

(1-a; 2-b; 3-b; 4-a; 5-b)

THE LANGUAGE OF TECHNOLOGY, SCIENCE, AND MEDICINE

access code   password allowing entry into a computer

acclimate   to accustom to a new environment

acid rain   excessively acidic precipitation due to industrial pollutants

acoustic   pertaining to hearing or with sound

acupressure   massage technique using acupuncture points; shiatsu

aerobics   vigorous exercise promoting cardiovascular health

aftershock   smaller tremors following main earthquake shock

agglomerate   to form into a ball; to gather into one mass

AI   artificial intelligence

AIDS   acquired immune deficiency syndrome—a complex condition caused by the HIV virus, which destroys the body's ability to fight infections

algorithm   formula for solving a particular problem

anatomy   study of the structure of living organisms

antigen   foreign substance against which the body produces an antibody

biodegradable   capable of being broken down and absorbed within a natural environment

bionics   design of systems that duplicate living organisms

biosphere   ecosphere; area of Earth in which living organisms can be supported

biotechnology   applications of genetic research such as cloning, recombinant DNA, and genetic engineering

breeder reactor   nuclear reactor that produces more fissionable material than it consumes

catalyst   substance that causes change in other substances without itself being affected

CD-ROM   compact disc read-only memory; used for permanent storage of massive amounts of information

congenital   condition, usually inherited, present at birth

CPR   cardiopulmonary resuscitation

cybernetics   science of communication and information theory

cyberspace   virtual reality

download   receive data on one's computer from a bulletin board service, mainframe, or network

DTP   desktop publishing

ecology   study of the interrelationship between living organisms and their environment

endogenous   developing from within; originating internally

epidemiology   study of the existence and spread of disease within a population

ergonomics	science concerned with developing safe machines for humans
etiology	cause of a specific disease
exogenous	developing from without; originating externally
fax	facsimile; phototelegraphy
fiber optics	technology that uses glass threads to transmit data
floppy disk	portable soft magnetic disk used for storing computer data
genealogy	science or study of family descent
geriatrics	treatment of the disorders of old age
greenhouse effect	increase of carbon dioxide in the Earth's atmosphere which, by interfering with the dissipation of normal radiant heat, raises its temperature
hard disk	magnetic disk used to store computer data; a hard disk holds more data and is faster than a floppy disk
herbivorous	feeding plants
hydrous	containing water, esp. water of crystallization or hydration, as in certain mineral and chemical compounds
hypertension	abnormally high blood pressure or a disease of which it is the chief sign

igneous	produced by the action of fire; specif. formed by volcanic action or intense heat, as rocks solidified from molten magma at or below the surface of the earth
indigenous	existing, growing, or produced naturally in a region or country; belonging as a native
intravenous	in, or directly into, a vein or veins
irradiate	to heat with radiant energy
kinesiology	principles and mechanics of human movement
laptop	small and portable computer
Lyme disease	form of arthritis caused by a bacterium carried by deer ticks
metamorphose	to change in form or nature; transform
metastasis	spread of a tumor from its original site throughout the body
MIS	management information system
modem	device that enables computers to transmit data over telephone lines
network	group of two or more linked computer systems
notebook	extremely lightweight personal computer
olfactory	having to do with the sense of smell
oncology	study and treatment of tumors

on-line   turned on and connected, in reference to computers

pathogen   microorganism that produces a specific disease

permutation   any radical alteration; total transformation

RAM   random access memory, the most common type of memory found in computers

robotics   area of computer science creating robots; branch of artificial intelligence (AI)

software   computer instructions or data; program to enable computer use

soporific   tending to or causing sleep

subcutaneous   being used or introduced beneath the skin

technology   application of science to practical affairs

teleshopping   electronic shopping via videotex

tsunami   tidal wave

upload   transmit data from a computer to a bulletin board service, mainframe, or network

user-friendly easy to understand and use without extensive training

vertex   top, highest point, apex, zenith

vestige   trace, mark, or sign of something that once existed but has passed away or disappeared

viability   capacity to live and continue normal development

videotex   transmission of data over telephone lines for display on video terminals

voice mail   electronic system for recording, storage, and retrieval of voice messages

voice recognition area of computer science that designs computer systems to recognize spoken words

whitespace   all the characters that appear as blanks on a display screen or printer

word processing   use of computers to produce, edit, and print documents

Drill 50

Match the word on the left with its definition in the right-hand column.

1. exogenous	a. containing water
2. hydrous	b. design of systems duplicating living organisms
3. pathogen	c. communication and information theory
4. bionics	d. originating externally
5. cybernetics	e. disease-producing microorganism
6. etiology	f. study of human movement
7. geriatrics	g. cause of specific disease
8. cyberspace	h. tidal wave
9. kinesiology	i. virtual reality
10. tsunami	j. treatment of old-age disorders

(1-d; 2-a; 3-e; 4-b; 5-c; 6-g; 7-j; 8-i; 9-f; 10-h)

Drill 51

Match each term on the right with its definition in the left-hand column.

1. red blood cell
2. diseased itching
3. nerve pain
4. removal of womb
5. inflammation of inner heart lining

a. endocarditis
b. hysterectomy
c. psoriasis
d. erythrocyte
e. neuralgia

(1-d; 2-c; 3-e; 4-b; 5-a)

THE LANGUAGE OF BUSINESS, SOCIETY, AND POLITICS

abdicate
to give up formally a high office, throne, or authority

acquisition
purchase of a company and control of its stock

adjourn
to close a session or meeting for a time

affirmative action
program to increase the proportion of women and minorities in the private and public sectors

affluence
wealth and economic power

agribusiness
production and marketing of agricultural products by large corporations instead of by individual farmers

AMEX
American Stock Exchange

amnesty
general pardon, esp. for political offenses against a government

amortization
process of extinguishing debt, usually by equal payments at regular intervals over time

anarchy
absence of government

annuity
payment of a fixed sum of money at regular intervals of time, esp. yearly

arbitrage
simultaneous buying and selling of large quantities of stocks in different markets to take advantage of price differences

bear market
declining stock market

bedroom community   suburb

beneficiary   anyone receiving benefit or inheritance

bloc   group of voters who vote together because of a common bond

bourse   stock exchange in a European city

bull market   improving trends in a stock market

buyout   purchase of a controlling share of a company

cadre   basic structure or framework; nucleus, core group

CD   certificate of deposit

censure   judgment or resolution condemning a person for misconduct

clan   extended family

collateral   side by side, parallel; securities for a debt

commonweal   general welfare

covert   hidden, secret, concealed; disguised; surreptitious

delegate   person authorized or sent to speak and act for others; representative

demagogue   person who tries to stir up the people by appeals to emotion and prejudice to win them over quickly and so gain power

democracy   majority rule; government of and by the people

dividend	portion of corporate profits distributed to shareholders
edict	official public proclamation or order issued by authority; decree
EEC	European Economic Community; formerly called the Common Market
emissary	person or agent sent on a specific mission
enterprise zone	location in which government seeks to stimulate new business enterprises by providing financial incentives
entitlement program	government program that pays benefits to those who meet whatever eligibility standards are established
ESOP	employee stock ownership plan
forecast	analysis and prediction of market trends
geopolitics	study of the relationship between geography and the relations among nations
global village	concept of the world as a single community due to mass communication and rapid transportation
GNP	gross national product
IMF	International Monetary Fund
interdict	to prohibit an action or the use of; to forbid with authority

legislature	body of persons given the responsibility and power to make laws for a country or state
liquidity	ease of converting an investment into cash
magnate	very important or influential person in any field of activity, esp. in a large business
malfeasance	wrongdoing or misconduct, esp. by a public official
market research	gathering and analysis of information on consumer habits, preferences, and trends
matriarch	woman who is head of a family or tribe
megalopolis	heavily populated area encompassing several cities
mores	ways that are considered conducive to the welfare of society and so, through general observance, develop the force of law, often becoming part of the formal legal code
mutual funds	mutually owned funds invested in diversified securities
NASDAQ	National Association of Securities Dealers Automated Quotations
nepotism	granting of political favors to relatives
NYSE	New York Stock Exchange
partisan	person who takes the part of or strongly supports one side, party, or person
patriarch	man who is head of a family or tribe

pluralism	existence of diverse cultural groups within a society
plutocracy	government by the wealthy
principal	face amount of a loan, excluding interest
profit margin	remaining income after expenses and costs
prospectus	statement outlining the main features of a new work or business enterprise, or the attractions of an established institution
protocol	code of ceremonial forms and courtesies accepted as proper and correct in official dealings, as between heads of states or diplomatic officials
quorum	minimum number of members that must be present for an assembly to conduct business
quotation	current price of security or commodity
risk management	conserving assets by controlling the uncertainty of financial loss
schism	split or division in an organized group or society, esp. a church, as the result of difference of opinion or doctrine
SEC	Securities and Exchange Commission, federal agency regulating stock and commodities markets
secular trend	long-term direction of economy

socioeconomic involving the interrelationship of social and economic factors

spin doctor political spokesperson who promotes a favorable interpretation of events to journalists

stratocracy government by the military

trust arrangement in which property is held by a person or corporation for the benefit of others

yield percentage of money returned on an investment

young Turks any new or young members of an organization who seek to change or reform it

zero-base budgeting starting to calculate a new budget from zero

Drill 52

Match each word on the left with its definition in the right-hand column.

1. dividend	a. political favors for relatives
2. nepotism	b. stock exchange in Europe
3. bourse	c. purchase of controlling share of company
4. cadre	d. profits distributed to shareholders
5. buyout	e. basic structure or framework

(1-d; 2-a; 3-b; 4-e; 5-c)

Drill 53

Choose the word or phrase that best completes the meaning of the sentence.

1. The convicted criminal was _____ at the federal prison.
   a. incarcerated   c. indicted
   b. extradited   d. intestate

2. To be legally insane or incompetent is to be _____.
   a. *nolo contendere*   c. *pro bono publico*
   c. *non compos mentis*   d. *corpus delicti*

3. The consumer _____ division of the attorney general's office tries to protect innocent people from the deceptive promises and defective products of unscrupulous salespeople.
   a. litigation   c. fraud
   b. tort   d. larceny

4. Only a professional surveyor can determine the exact boundary of _____ pieces of property.
   a. abjure   c. intestate
   b. probate   d. contiguous

5. When you take out a loan to purchase a new car, the bank has a(n) _____ on the car.
   a. fraud   c. inquest
   b. libel   d. lien

(1-a; 2-b; 3-c; 4-d; 5-d)

Drill 54

Choose the word or phrase that means most nearly the same as the *italicized* word.

1. *obfuscate*
   a. temporize
   b. complete
   c. confuse
   d. reuse

2. *ostentatious*
   a. pretentious
   b. deep voiced
   c. animated
   d. retiring

3. *panacea*
   a. illogical statement
   b. tranquility
   c. cure-all
   d. belief in God

4. *paradigm*
   a. model
   b. puzzle
   c. seizure
   d. cure-all

5. *paraphrase*
   a. quote
   b. joke
   c. rewording
   d. attribution

6. *partisan*
   a. devoted to a cause
   b. many-colored
   c. dubious
   d. fragmented

7. *pedantic*
   a. hiker
   b. extravagantly wealthy
   c. intellectual showing-off
   d. jaywalker

8. *penurious*
   a. stingy
   b. slow-moving
   c. ancient
   d. happy-go-lucky

9. *peremptory*
   a. judicial
   b. decreed
   c. imperative
   d. unnecessary

10. *permeable*
    a. penetrable by fluids
    b. transferrable
    c. translucent
    d. impervious

(1-c; 2-a; 3-c; 4-a; 5-c; 6-a; 7-c; 8-c; 9-c; 10-a)

Drill 55

Match each term on the left with its definition in the right-hand column.

1. arteriosclerosis
2. cyanosis
3. encephalogram
4. bradycardia
5. quadraplegia

a. abnormally slow heartbeat
b. paralysis of four limbs
c. hardening of the arteries
d. brain wave measurement
e. bluish skin condition

(1-c; 2-e; 3-d; 4-a; 5-b)

ESSENTIAL VOCABULARY V

S

salacious	obscene
salient	conspicuous, noticeable, prominent
sanctimony	affected piety or righteousness; religious hypocrisy
sardonic	ironical, sarcastic
satiate	to satisfy to the fullest
secular	not sacred or religious
sedulous	diligent, working hard and steadily
sentient	conscious; intelligent; able to perceive
sequester	to set apart, separate, segregate
simultaneous	occurring or existing at the same time
sinecure	job requiring little actual work
solicitude	care for or concern about someone
somatic	pertaining to the body
sonorous	sounds having full, deep, or rich quality
specious	plausible but not true
spurious	false; counterfeit
statute	formal regulation
stoic	showing austere indifference to emotion
stratagem	trick, scheme, or plan for deceiving
strident	harsh-sounding, shrill, grating
stringent	severe, strict
subterfuge	deception; plan, action, or device used to hide one's true objective
subversive	causing to subvert, overthrow, or destroy

succinct   terse; to the point

suffuse   to overspread; to fill with

supercilious   disdainful, contemptuous; haughty

superfluous   more than is needed, surplus

supersede   to take the place of; to overrule

supplicate   to ask for humbly

surfeit   excess of something

surreptitious   acting in a secret, stealthy way

synthesis   putting together parts to form a whole

Drill 56

Choose the word or phrase that means most nearly the same as the *italicized* word.

1. supercilious
  a. absentminded
  b. haughty
  c. punctual
  d. jovial

2. salacious
  a. mouth-watering
  b. vegetarian
  c. illegal
  d. obscene

3. surreptitious
  a. sleeping
  b. clandestine
  c. flawed
  d. careful

4. tacitly
  a. politely
  b. with few words
  c. stealthily
  d. by implication

5. temporize
  a. count
  b. delay
  c. order
  d. select

6. terse
  a. loquacious
  b. mumbled
  c. to the point
  d. harmonious

7. succinct
  a. satisfying
  b. voluptuous
  c. hollowed
  d. terse

8. transitory
  a. affixed
  b. fleeting
  c. dreamy
  d. crosswise

9. tenet
  a. assistant
  b. renter
  c. dome
  d. doctrine

10. tribulation
  a. acclaim
  b. great trouble
  c. great reward
  d. branching out

(1-b; 2-d; 3-b; 4-d; 5-b; 6-c; 7-d; 8-b; 9-d; 10-b)

T

tacit	unspoken, unexpressed, implied
tangential	diverging, digressing
tangible	able to be touched or felt; having form and substance
tedious	boring; wearisome, tiresome
temporize	to act relevant to the circumstances, rather than to principle; to draw out in order to gain time
tenable	able to be held, defended, or maintained
tenacity	perseverance; firmness
tenet	doctrine, belief
tenuous	not secure or substantial; slight, flimsy
terminate	to bring to an end
terse	briefly and succinctly stated
torpid	slow, dull, apathetic
tractable	easily managed
transcendent	beyond the limits of possible experience
transcribe	to write or type out in full
transgression	breach of a law, duty, or responsibility
transitory	fleeting, not durable or long-lasting
transmute	to change form
transverse	to pass or extend over or through
trauma	wound or injury
trenchant	keen, incisive; penetrating
trepidation	fearful uncertainty, anxiety, apprehension
tribulation	great sadness, misery, or distress
truculent	cruel, savage; scathingly harsh

truncate	to shorten, edit
turbulent	stirred-up; full of commotion
turgid	swollen, distended
turpitude	vileness, depravity

Drill 57

Choose the word that best completes the meaning of the sentence.

1. The fortune-teller's predictions were _____, although uncanny.
   a. salacious   c. strident
   b. specious   d. sonorous

2. Please summarize the most _____ points at the beginning of the report.
   a. salacious   c. salient
   b. secular   d. stoic

3. The carnival barker's voice was _____ and startling.
   a. strident   c. spurious
   b. stringent   d. somatic

4. The room was _____ with the pink glow of early morning.
   a. surfeit   c. suffused
   b. supplicated   d. superseded

5. To apologize again is _____. I have already forgotten the remark you made.
   a. subversive   c. supercilious
   b. surreptitious   d. superfluous

(1-b; 2-c; 3-a; 4-c; 5-d)

Drill 58

Match the word on the left with its definition in the right-hand column.

1. demagoguery
2. quotation
3. annuity
4. plutocracy
5. entitlement program

a. fixed sum of money paid at intervals
b. stirring people up by appealing to emotions
c. paying benefits according to eligibility standards
d. current price of stock or commodity
e. government by the wealthy

(1-b; 2-d; 3-a; 4-e; 5-c)

U

ubiquitous	omnipresent; seeming to be everywhere at the same time
umbrage	offense, resentment
uncanny	mysterious, eerie, weird
uncouth	gauche, awkward; unrefined
undulating	moving sinuously, wave-like
unethical	without principles, unscrupulous
uniform	consistent, the same throughout
unilateral	involving only one of several parties; not reciprocal
unmitigated	not lessened or eased; full-forced
unprecedented	previously unheard-of; without model or previous example
unscrupulous	unprincipled; not ruled by morals or ethics
unwieldy	awkward or cumbersome to handle
upbraid	to criticize
urbane	polished and refined; courteous
usurp	to seize a government or power unlawfully

V

vacillate	to be inconstant, wavering, or unsteady
vacuous	showing lack of intelligence or sense; empty; inane
vanquish	to conquer, overcome
vapid	tasteless, flat; uninteresting, boring
variable	changeable, fluctuating, not constant
variegated	diverse, full of differences or variation

vendetta	blood feud
verbatim	word for word
verbose	wordy, long-winded, prolix
verisimilitude	appearance of being true and real
verity	truthfulness, honesty, actuality
vernacular	native language of a locale
viability	capability to survive
vicarious	experienced through imagined participation in another person's experiences
vicissitudes	unpredictable ups and downs of circumstance
vigilant	watchful, alert
vilification	abusive or slanderous language; defamation
vindicate	to clear of guilt or blame
vindictive	vengeful; unforgiving
vociferous	loud, vehement, clamorous; very assertive
volatile	unstable, mercurial; explosive
volition	conscious and deliberate decision and action
voracious	insatiable; very hungry

Drill 59

Choose the word or phrase that means most nearly the same as the *italicized* word.

1. *quintessence*
   a. royalty
   b. forgetfulness
   c. superciliousness
   d. example

2. *umbrage*
   a. cloudiness
   b. touchiness
   c. spreading out
   d. rank growth

3. *unilateral*
   a. one-level
   b. wholesome
   c. undivided
   d. one-sided

4. *unprecedented*
   a. not planned
   b. never done before
   c. without warning
   d. totally forgotten

5. *vacillation*
   a. prevention
   b. whiskers
   c. fluttering in the wind
   d. fluctuation of mind

6. *vendetta*
   a. shade
   b. carriage
   c. blood feud
   d. celebration

7. *verbose*
   a. wordy
   b. hand-written
   c. terse
   d. eloquent

8. *voracious*
   a. furious
   b. empty
   c. hungry
   d. very loud

9. *viability*
   a. capacity to live
   b. ability to laugh
   c. true-to-life
   d. capacity

10. *vicissitudes*
   a. likeness
   b. misery
   c. ups and downs
   d. foresightedness

(1-d; 2-b; 3-d; 4-b; 5-d; 6-c; 7-a; 8-c; 9-a; 10-c)

Drill 60

Choose the word that best completes the meaning of the sentence.

1. A true survivor is one with the _____ to keep on going, no matter what.
   a. termination   c. torpidity
   c. tenacity   d. temporizing

2. Many minimum-wage jobs are _____ and unfulfilling.
   a. transitory   c. transcendent
   b. terse   d. tedious

3. The waters were far too _____ for canoeing with the children.
   a. truculent   c. turgid
   b. trenchant   d. turbulent

4. The clowns were _____; everywhere we turned, there was another one smiling.
   a. ubiquitous   c. urbane
   b. undulating   d. uncouth

5. An _____ salesperson will quickly lose any repeat business.
   a. unmitigated   c. unscrupulous
   b. uncanny   d. unilateral

W

wager	to bet
waive	to give up a right, claim, or privilege
wan	pale, weak, listless
warp	to twist, bend
warrant	to deserve; to justify
wary	distrustful
weld	to unite by heating
wheedle	to implore with flattery or coaxing
wield	to handle, use, control
wily	sly, cunning, crafty
wince	to shrink back; to flinch
winnow	to sift through in order to separate
wont	usual habit, custom
wraithlike	ghostlike; very pale
wrest	to grab away; to seize

Y

yearn	to pine away for; to long for, desire strongly
yelp	short, sharp cry of pain
yield	(*v.*) to give over, relinquish (*n.*) harvest, product, or return on investment
yowl	long wailing cry, howl

Z

zany	clownish, ludicrous
zeal	intense enthusiasm, earnestness
zenith	point directly overhead; the highest point

Drill 61

Choose the word or phrase that means most nearly the same as the *italicized* word.

1. urbane
 a. street-wise
 b. ignorant
 c. refined
 d. foolish

2. retroactive
 a. effective earlier
 b. returnable
 c. diminishing
 d. spiraling

3. vacuous
 a. whirling
 b. puffed out
 c. senseless
 d. leafy

4. secular
 a. not religious
 b. naval
 c. sanctimonious
 d. unorthodox

5. simultaneous
 a. chronological
 b. temporal
 c. at the same time
 d. permanent

6. sonorous
 a. resonant
 b. snoring
 c. whispered
 d. silent

7. stoic
 a. frivolous
 b. morbid
 c. calmly strong
 d. worried

8. stringent
 a. strict
 b. brisk
 c. long-legged
 d. gregarious

9. subterfuge
 a. beneath the rose
 b. underground
 c. deception
 d. submerged

10. usurp
 a. seize
 b. belch
 c. translate
 d. suppress

(1-c; 2-a; 3-c; 4-a; 5-c; 6-a; 7-c; 8-a; 9-c; 10-a)

Drill 62

Choose the word that best completes the meaning of the sentence.

1. As the barricades went up, the partisans understood the gravity and _____ of the situation.
   a. verbatim
   b. volatility
   c. vacuousness
   d. vacillation

2. Many parents live _____ through their children.
   a. vicariously
   b. vindictively
   c. verity
   d. vacuously

3. You must choose of your own _____; no one should force you into a decision.
   a. verbosity
   b. vicissitudes
   c. volition
   d. verisimilitude

4. As was her _____, she took a five-mile walk before breakfast each day.
   a. wraith
   b. warp
   c. wont
   d. weld

5. The young actor was jubilant, having reached the _____ of his career.
   a. zenith
   b. winnow
   c. apotheosis
   d. nadir

(1-b; 2-a; 3-c; 4-c; 5-a)

6

Fine-tuning
Final Challenges

No language so rich and dynamic as English could possibly have a simple system of rules for its spelling, grammar, and syntax. Because of its melting-pot history and rapid development, it does have a rather irregular — and sometimes frustrating — set of rules (and exceptions to those rules).

However, you do not need an extensive review of grammar to master some of the most common stumbling blocks to effective spoken and written communication. In Chapter 6 you will learn some unique methods and "tricks of the trade" that will greatly increase your confidence, now that you have mastered so many words. These are the final bits of polishing that will perfect your communication skills.

PROBLEMS WITH VERB FORMS

The following irregular (or *strong*) verb forms frequently confuse people. As their forms change without a predictable pattern, you would do well to remember them.

Present	Past	Past Participle
awake	awoke	(have) awoken
bid	bade	(have) bidden
bind	bound	(have) bound
bite	bit	(have) bitten
blow	blew	(have) blown
break	broke	(have) broken
cleave	cleft	(have) cloven
dive	dove	(have) dived
draw	drew	(have) drawn
fly	flew	(have) flown
forsake	forsook	(have) forsaken
lay	laid	(have) laid
leave	left	(have) left
lie	lay	(have) lain
melt	melted	(have) molten
mow	mowed	(have) mown
rise	rose	(have) risen
shave	shaved	(have) shaven
show	showed	(have) shown
slay	slew	(have) slain
strike	struck	(have) stricken
swear	swore	(have) sworn
tear	tore	(have) torn
tread	trod	(have) trodden

Drill 63

Fill in the correct forms of the following verbs.

Present	Past	Past Participle
1. _____	awoke	_____
2. bid	_____	_____
3. _____	_____	have bound
4. _____	bit	_____
5. blow	_____	_____
6. _____	_____	have broken
7. dive	_____	_____
8. _____	_____	have drawn
9. fly	_____	_____
10. _____	_____	have laid

(See page 195 for answers.)

Drill 64

Fill in the correct forms of the following verbs.

Present	Past	Past Participle
1. _____	left	_____
2. _____	_____	have lain
3. melt	_____	_____
4. _____	_____	have mown
5. _____	rose	_____
6. _____	_____	have shaven
7. slay	_____	_____
8. _____	struck	_____
9. _____	_____	have sworn
10. tear	_____	_____

(See page 195 for answers.)

IRREGULAR AND UNUSUAL PLURALS

In English, almost all nouns form the plural by adding "s": boy, boys. But there are several groups of nouns that don't quite follow that rule. For example, there are words that have no singular form, yet have a plural: pants. Others that have no plural form often have a singular: music. There's another group called collective nouns which imply a plural—more than one—yet take a singular verb: jury. And then there are the irregular plurals: ox, oxen.

Drill 65

The following words do not conform to regular rules for creating plurals. Provide the correct singular or plural form (where possible) and then assign each word to one of the following categories:

irregular; collective; no singular; no plural

1. committee/_____ _____
2. child/_____ _____
3. cattle/_____ _____
4. wheat/_____ _____
5. trousers/_____ _____
6. louse/_____ _____
7. class/_____ _____
8. team/_____ _____
9. scissors/_____ _____
10. courage/_____ _____
11. goose/_____ _____
12. crew/_____ _____
13. deer/_____ _____
14. crowd/_____ _____
15. billiards/_____ _____
16. shears/_____ _____
17. army/_____ _____
18. brother/_____ _____
19. sheep/_____ _____
20. pliers/_____ _____

(See page 196 for answers.)

PROBLEM WORD PAIRS

When is it correct to use *accompanied with* as opposed to *accompanied by?* What's the difference in meaning between *cannon* and *canon?* Why is it incorrect to use *anticipate* when you mean *expect?* Is that word spelled *beseige* or *besiege?* Having powerful communication skills demands precise and skillful use of such fine points of expression in both verbal and written communication.

ability (skill)	vs.	**capacity** (aptitude)
accompanied with (referring to objects)	vs.	**accompanied by** (referring to persons)
accountable for (referring to actions)	vs.	**accountable to** (referring to persons)
adverse to (unfavorable)	vs.	**averse to** (reluctant)
advice (noun: wise suggestion)	vs.	**advise** (verb: to counsel)
affect (to influence or change)	vs.	**effect** (verb: to bring about noun: result)
aggravate (to make worse)	vs.	**irritate** (to annoy)
agree to (to consent to)	vs.	**agree with** (to be in accord with)
aid (assistance)	vs.	**aide** (assistant)
allusion (indirect reference)	vs.	**illusion** (false idea or unreal image)
allusion (indirect reference)	vs.	**reference** (direct mention)
altar (noun: religious platform)	vs.	**alter** (verb: to change)

altogether (completely)   vs.   **all together** (all at one time)

ambiguous (not clear, vague, unintentionally confusing)   vs.   **equivocal** (purposely vague, intentionally confusing)

among (referring to more than two)   vs.   **between** (referring to two)

anticipate (to expect and prepare for)   vs.   **expect** (to look forward to)

anxious (uneasy, apprehensive, worried)   vs.   **eager** (feeling keen desire, impatient to do or get)

assume (to take for granted, suppose)   vs.   **presume** (to accept as true, lacking proof to the contrary)

avenge (to punish justly)   vs.   **revenge** (to retaliate)

bad (adjective)   vs.   **badly** (adverb)

bate (to lessen force of)   vs.   **bait** (to lure, tease, torment)

beside (at the side of)   vs.   **besides** (in addition to)

bloc (alliance)   vs.   **block** (cube)

bring (to me)   vs.   **take** (from me)

callus (painful growth on foot)   vs.   **callous** (lacking pity, insensitive)

cannon (weapon)   vs.   **canon** (law or rule)

canvas (noun: heavy cloth)   vs.   **canvass** (verb: to examine in detail, survey)

capital (money; chief)   vs.   **capitol** (building; city)

ceremonial (pertaining to things) vs. **ceremonious** (pertaining to both things and people)

cite (verb: to refer to) vs. **site** (noun: location)

coarse (adjective: rough) vs. **course** (noun: path)

compare to (pertaining to similarities) vs. **compare with** (pertaining to both similarities and differences)

complacent (self-satisfied, smug) vs. **complaisant** (willing to please, obliging)

complement (that which completes) vs. **compliment** (expression of courtesy or respect)

comprise (to include, consist of: parts embracing whole) vs. **composed of** (to make up or constitute: whole embracing parts)

consists of (to be formed or composed of parts) vs. **consists in** (to be inherent in something)

continual (happening over and over, at intervals) vs. **continuous** (going on uninterrupted)

contrast to (pertaining to opposites) vs. **contrast with** (pertaining to differences)

councilor (member of council) vs. **counselor** (one who counsels, gives advice)

cynical (sarcastic, sneering) vs. **skeptical** (not easily persuaded, doubting)

definite (precise and clear in meaning) vs. **definitive** (decisive, conclusive)

denote (to refer to explicitly) vs. **connote** (to suggest, imply)

descent (noun: downward movement) vs. **dissent** (verb: to disagree)

desert (verb: abandon noun: arid region) vs. **dessert** (noun: sweet served as final meal course)

different from (pertaining to direct contrast) vs. **different than** (pertaining to degrees of difference)

differs from (pertaining to dissimilarities) vs. **differs with** (pertaining to a disagreement)

discreet (prudent, careful) vs. **discrete** (separate, distinct)

disinterested (impartial, unbiased) vs. **uninterested** (indifferent)

each other (used to indicate two members) vs. **one another** (used to indicate three or more)

egoism (self-interested, self-centered) vs. **egotism** (constant reference to self)

elder (referring to persons) vs. **older** (referring to things)

eminent (distinguished) vs. **imminent** (about to happen)

enhance (to highlight) vs. **improve** (to make better)

envy (discontent or resentment because of someone else's advantage) vs. **jealousy** (suspicion of rivalry)

especially (particularly) vs. **specially** (for a specific reason)

explicit (stated plainly) vs. **implicit** (understood)

farther (pertaining to distance) vs. **further** (pertaining to time or degree)

feasible (capable of being done) vs. **possible** (capable of existing or happening)

fewer (referring to number) vs. **less** (referring to amount)

flaunt (to make a conspicuous or defiant display) vs. **flout** (to mock or scoff at, show contempt for)

forebear (noun: ancestor) vs. **forbear** (verb: to endure, tolerate)

formally (in a formal manner) vs. **formerly** (previously)

former (that mentioned first) vs. **latter** (that mentioned second)

forward (moving ahead) vs. **foreword** (introductory remark, preface)

founder (to stumble, sink) vs. **flounder** (to struggle, speak awkwardly)

gourmet (person who is an excellent judge of fine foods and drinks, epicure) vs. **gourmand** (person with a heavy appetite in excess)

grateful to (referring to person) vs. **grateful for** (referring to things)

hanged (pertaining to a person) vs. **hung** (pertaining to an object)

homogeneous (similar or identical) vs. **homogenous** (similar in structure; uniform)

human (pertaining to the human race) vs. **humane** (compassionate)

imminent (impending)	vs.	**eminent** (lofty, distinguished, outstanding)
imply (to hint, suggest)	vs.	**infer** (to conclude, deduce)
incredible (unbelievable)	vs.	**incredulous** (unbelieving)
ingenious (clever, inventive)	vs.	**ingenuous** (open, candid, without guile)
later (referring to time)	vs.	**latter** (the second of two items named)
lay (takes an object)	vs.	**lie** (does not take an object)
lessen (verb: to decrease)	vs.	**lesson** (noun: school study material)
lightening (form of the verb "to brighten")	vs.	**lightning** (flash of light)
like it was (used in informal speech)	vs.	**as if it were** (used in formal speech)
loath (adverb: unwilling, reluctant)	vs.	**loathe** (verb: to feel intense dislike or disgust, detest)
loose (adverb: not tight)	vs.	**lose** (verb: to misplace something)
maybe (adverb: perhaps)	vs.	**may be** (verb: could be)
moral (adjective: ethical noun: ethical lesson)	vs.	**morale** (noun: spirit)
nauseous (adverb: sickening, disgusting)	vs.	**nauseated** (verb: to feel sick)

noisome (harmful, foul-smelling)   vs.   **noisy** (loud)

parameter (constant)   vs.   **perimeter** (outer boundary)

perquisite (tip, privilege, benefit)   vs.   **prerequisite** (something required beforehand)

perspective (noun: a specific viewpoint)   vs.   **prospective** (adjective: expected, future)

pertinent (relevant)   vs.   **pertaining** (associated with, relative to)

practicable (can be put into practice)   vs.   **practical** (sensible, utilitarian)

precipitate (verb: to bring on; to hasten)   vs.   **precipitous** (adverb: steep)

preclude (to make impossible or unnecessary)   vs.   **prevent** (to stop from happening)

principal (first in rank, authority, importance)   vs.   **principle** (fundamental truth or law)

proceed (to advance, move forward)   vs.   **precede** (to come before)

proved (tested conclusively)   vs.   **proven** (tested by time)

publicity (has a positive connotation)   vs.   **notoriety** (has a negative connotation)

raise (takes an object)   vs.   **rise** (does not take an object)

reign (ruler's tenure on throne)   vs.   **rein** (leather strap)

repulse (to drive back)   vs.   **repel** (to disgust)

respectful (full of respect) vs. **respective** (in the order given)

reticent (silent, disinclined to talk) vs. **reluctant** (unwilling)

sensual (connected with sexual pleasure) vs. **sensuous** (appealing to the senses)

stationary (adverb: not moving, standing still) vs. **stationery** (noun: writing papers)

straight (adjective: not crooked) vs. **strait** (noun: difficulty, distress)

subsequently (afterward) vs. **consequently** (therefore)

that (used in a restrictive phrase) vs. **which** (used in a nonrestrictive phrase)

tortuous (full of twists and turns, windings) vs. **torturous** (very painful)

turbid (muddy, clouded, confused) vs. **turgid** (swollen)

unaware (unknowing) vs. **unawares** (caught by surprise)

unexceptional (ordinary) vs. **unexceptionable** (beyond criticism)

venal (capable of being bribed or corrupted) vs. **venial** (forgivable, pardonable)

who (referring to a person) vs. **that** (referring to either a person or thing)

vs. **which** (referring to a thing)

Drill 66

Choose the correct word to complete each of the following sentences.

1. She was _____ eating foods she was not familiar with.
   a. averse to   b. adverse to

2. Put the kerosene lamp _____ your sleeping bag before you go to sleep.
   a. besides   b. beside

3. The faucet dripped _____ all night.
   a. continuously   b. continually

4. He _____ his supervisor about how best to complete the project.
   a. differed with   b. differed from

5. My _____ brother has always enjoyed visiting with us on the holidays.
   a. elder   b. older

6. If you go _____ down the road, you'll see the museum on the left.
   a. further   b. farther

7. I am _____ to criticize someone who is learning a new skill.
   a. loathe   b. loath

8. A limousine is a _____ of the top executive.
   a. perquisite   b. prerequisite

9. You can use the high-quality company _____ for those important reports.
   a. stationary   b. stationery

10. The child was caught _____ with her hand in the cookie jar.

a. unawares   b. unaware

(1-a; 2-b; 3-a; 4-a; 5-a; 6-b; 7-b; 8-a; 9-b; 10-a)

DRILL ANSWERS

Answers for Drill 63 (page 181)

1.	awake	awoke	have awoken
2.	bid	bade	have bidden
3.	bind	bound	have bound
4.	bite	bit	have bitten
5.	blow	blew	have blown
6.	break	broke	have broken
7.	dive	dove	have dived
8.	draw	drew	have drawn
9.	fly	flew	have flown
10.	lay	laid	have laid

Answers for Drill 64 (page 182)

1.	leave	left	have left
2.	lie	lay	have lain
3.	melt	melted	have melted
4.	mow	mowed	have mown
5.	rise	rose	have risen
6.	shave	shaved	have shaven
7.	slay	slew	have slain
8.	strike	struck	have stricken
9.	swear	swore	have sworn
10.	tear	tore	have torn

Answers for Drill 65 (page 184)

Irregular Plurals	*Collective Nouns*
child/children	committee
louse/lice	class
goose/geese	team
brother/brethren	crew
	crowd
	army

Nouns with No Singular	*Nouns with No Plural*
trousers	cattle
scissors	wheat
billiards	courage
shears	deer
pliers	sheep

Review Drills

Drill 67

Choose the word or phrase that means most nearly the same as the *italicized* word.

1. *abet*
   a. encourage crime
   b. gamble
   c. shorten
   d. curse

2. *abeyance*
   a. distance
   b. leave-taking
   c. postponement
   d. hatred

3. *acolyte*
   a. painter
   b. volcanic
   c. bejeweled
   d. assistant

4. *abnegate*
   a. forget
   b. deny
   c. prevent
   d. damage

5. *abortive*
   a. stuttering
   b. illegal
   c. deadening
   d. ineffectual

6. *abridge*
   a. cross over
   b. shorten
   c. extend
   d. circumvent

7. *abscond*
   a. forgive
   b. abstain
   c. cut and slash
   d. steal and flee

8. *accolade*
   a. musical
   b. award
   c. unpleasant
   d. steep incline

9. *accede*
   a. proceed
   b. precede
   c. prevent
   d. consent

10. *adipose*
    a. reclining
    b. fatty
    c. demanding
    d. superficial

(1-a; 2-c; 3-d; 4-b; 5-d; 6-b; 7-d; 8-b; 9-d; 10-b)

Drill 68

Choose the word or phrase that means most nearly the same as the *italicized* word.

1. *consign*
   a. loan to
   b. trust to
   c. claim for
   d. denounce

2. *candor*
   a. rudeness
   b. rancor
   c. frankness
   d. stealth

3. *codicil*
   a. sworn statement
   b. mortgage
   c. co-signed loan
   d. amendment to will

4. *capitol*
   a. wealth
   b. investment
   c. headquarters
   d. building

5. *capitulate*
   a. surrender
   b. decapitate
   c. invest
   d. demand

6. *carnal*
   a. of the body
   b. of the heart
   c. of the spirit
   d. of the mind

7. *castigate*
   a. chatter
   b. encourage
   c. criticize
   d. shut tight

8. *cede*
   a. lease
   b. acknowledge
   c. follow
   d. yield

9. *celerity*
   a. swiftness
   b. infamy
   c. wittiness
   d. acidity

10. *chagrin*
    a. leer
    b. erratic
    c. skilled
    d. frustration

(1-b; 2-c; 3-d; 4-d; 5-a; 6-a; 7-c; 8-d; 9-a; 10-d)

Drill 69

Choose the word or phrase that means most nearly the same as the *italicized* word.

1. *choleric*
   a. smug
   b. angry
   c. pale
   d. diseased

2. *debauch*
   a. dehydrate
   b. steal away
   c. remove
   d. corrupt

3. *epithet*
   a. tombstone
   b. nickname
   c. spittle
   d. impediment

4. *deduce*
   a. lead away
   b. reason
   c. topple
   d. confuse

5. *deference*
   a. indifference
   b. mockery
   c. removal
   d. respect

6. *degenerate*
   a. destitute
   b. decline
   c. debilitate
   d. devolve

7. *enigma*
   a. birthmark
   b. disagreement
   c. abyss
   d. riddle

8. *exigency*
   a. way out
   b. necessity
   c. ambulatory
   d. opening

9. *demote*
   a. harmonize
   b. mobilize
   c. lower in rank
   d. raise in value

10. *denigrate*
    a. defame
    b. assign
    c. deny
    d. renounce

(1-b; 2-d; 3-b; 4-b; 5-d; 6-b; 7-d; 8-b; 9-c; 10-a)

Drill 70

Choose the word or phrase that means most nearly the same as the *italicized* word.

1. histrionic
   a. ancient
   b. infected
   c. theatrical
   d. depressing

2. peccadillo
   a. wild pig
   b. burrowing mammal
   c. mal
   d. petty fault

3. mitigate
   a. lessen
   b. incite
   c. measure
   d. prosecute

4. nebulous
   a. cloudy
   b. subdued
   c. awkward
   d. careless

5. laudable
   a. arrogant
   b. clean
   c. boisterous
   d. praiseworthy

6. impugn
   a. fool
   b. cast doubt
   c. make penniless
   d. ridicule

7. levity
   a. mediterranean
   b. floatable
   c. frivolity
   d. illumination

8. malign
   a. defame
   b. break
   c. separate
   d. injure

9. loquacious
   a. birdlike
   b. winding
   c. rich
   d. talkative

10. inveigh
   a. calculate
   b. forget
   c. argue
   d. remove

(1-c; 2-d; 3-a; 4-a; 5-d; 6-b; 7-c; 8-a; 9-d; 10-c)

Drill 71

Choose the word or phrase that means most nearly the same as the *italicized* word.

1. *jeopardy*
   a. cheerfulness
   b. banter
   c. risk
   d. feline

2. *nihilism*
   a. meaninglessness
   b. death
   c. socialism
   d. conversion

3. *materiel*
   a. fabric
   b. handmade
   c. equipment
   d. left-over

4. *libel*
   a. defamation
   b. inclination
   c. faint
   d. illegal transaction

5. *noxious*
   a. repulsive
   b. unkind
   c. injurious
   d. evil

6. *obliterate*
   a. demolish
   b. cloud
   c. forget
   d. read

7. *obscure*
   a. powerful
   b. threatening
   c. murky
   d. preoccupied

8. *obstreperous*
   a. boisterous
   b. infected
   c. stubborn
   d. uninvited

9. *obtuse*
   a. foreshortened
   b. frozen
   c. dull
   d. whirling

10. *onus*
    a. responsibility
    b. aperture
    c. exclamation
    d. monotone

(1-c; 2-a; 3-c; 4-a; 5-c; 6-a; 7-c; 8-a; 9-c; 10-a)

Drill 72

Choose the word or phrase that means most nearly the same as the *italicized* word.

1. *trauma*
   a. dream
   b. theatrics
   c. wounds
   d. depression

2. *supplicate*
   a. beg
   b. replace
   c. provide
   d. bend gently

3. *synthesis*
   a. phony
   b. collection
   c. combination of parts into whole
   d. splitting

4. *tedious*
   a. boring
   b. minute
   c. child-like
   d. melodious

5. *tenable*
   a. capable of being defended
   b. swift
   c. inhabitable
   d. capable of withstanding pain

6. *tractable*
   a. arable
   b. fertile
   c. easily led
   d. easily broken

7. *tacit*
   a. implied
   b. cheapened
   c. stitched
   d. moldy

8. *transmute*
   a. change direction
   b. change color
   c. change form
   d. change money

9. *trepidation*
   a. trembling
   b. fortitude
   c. stumbling
   d. hazard

10. *truncate*
    a. plant
    b. cut in pieces
    c. cut short
    d. put into containers

(1-c; 2-a; 3-c; 4-a; 5-a; 6-c; 7-a; 8-c; 9-a; 10-c)

Drill 73

Choose the word or phrase that means most nearly the same as the *italicized* word.

1. *ubiquitous*
   a. omnipresent
   b. impudent
   c. sinful
   d. curious

2. *undulating*
   a. softening
   b. splitting
   c. waving
   d. burying

3. *unmitigated*
   a. not lessened
   b. not sent
   c. without stop
   d. not understood

4. *vapid*
   a. bloodied
   b. frenetic
   c. dull
   d. countrified

5. *volatile*
   a. explosive
   b. musical
   c. dream-like
   d. truthful

6. *verbatim*
   a. forbidden
   b. paraphrased
   c. translated
   d. word for word

7. *verisimilitude*
   a. twinhood
   b. appearance of truth
   c. approaching
            perfection
   d. cheerfulness

8. *vindicate*
   a. accuse
   b. empty out
   c. release
   d. clear of blame

9. *vicarious*
   a. hilarious
   b. experienced
            secondhand
   c. remembered
   d. spiteful

10. *vilify*
    a. spy out
    b. spear through
    c. revitalize
    d. defame

(1-a; 2-c; 3-a; 4-c; 5-a; 6-d; 7-b; 8-d; 9-b; 10-d)

THE PRINCETON LANGUAGE INSTITUTE is a consortium of experts comprised of linguists, lexicographers, writers, teachers, and businesspeople. Applying academic rigor to practical endeavor, the Institute enables writers and members of professional communities to enhance their communication and language skills as they work to meet the challenges and complexities of the 21st century. The Princeton Language Institute is based in Princeton, New Jersey.

Printed in the United States
by Baker & Taylor Publisher Services